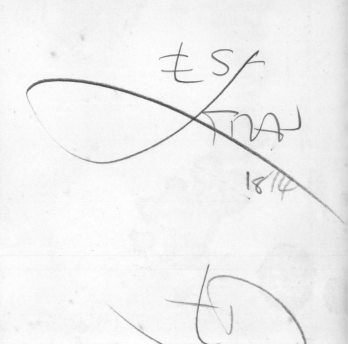

THE SHIP WITH TWO CAPTAINS

By the same author

THE GOLDEN HORSESHOE

WALKER, R.N.

THE TWO CAPTAINS
Jerauld Wright (*left*) and "Bill" Jewell.

THE SHIP WITH TWO CAPTAINS

by

TERENCE ROBERTSON

LONDON

EVANS BROTHERS LIMITED

First published 1957

Printed in Great Britain by
The Camelot Press Ltd., London and Southampton
Z. 5379

CONTENTS

ILLUSTRATIONS

*For permission to reproduce photographs in this book the publishers
are indebted to: The Admiralty; Imperial War Museum; Keystone
Press; and U.S. Army Signal Corps.*

FOREWORD BY THE TWO CAPTAINS

THE H.M.S. *Seraph* had as stirring and eminently successful a record as, I believe, any ship of any navy. I have a high regard for this splendid ship, her captain, officers and crew, and the organisation from which they came.

The two operations in which I participated aboard *Seraph* were among the first combined United States-United Kingdom tasks of the war. Particularly noteworthy was the splendid co-operation, warm friendship, and mutual understanding between all persons involved.

Looking back on these memorable events and ahead to the future, I am delighted that *Seraph's* special wartime missions, which contributed so much to the Allied cause, have been documented for all to read in *The Ship with Two Captains*.

Seraph's exploits set her apart. It is gratifying to know that she is still on active duty, and still under the over-all command of her first skipper, Captain Bill Jewell. But whether she is on the active list or not matters little, for in the minds and hearts of all who served in her the exploits of this fine ship and her splendid crew will live for all time.

JERAULD WRIGHT,
Admiral, U.S. Navy,
Supreme Allied Commander, Atlantic.

AS first Captain of the *Seraph* it was my good fortune that the submarine came to be chosen for the job of landing General Clark and his team of officers in North Africa for their conference with General Mast. This led to other special operations and, at the same time, gave my officers and myself the privilege of meeting and knowing a number of distinguished Americans who, as the author points out, are all now in high places. We, in the *Seraph* at the time, were much indebted to them for their many kind and thoughtful actions.

The submarine had many friends; first at Vickers-Arm-strongs, where she was built, and who were so helpful when asked to do any small thing; next the school children of Barrow-in-Furness, who adopted her, if not officially, at least with their many good wishes and gifts of books and sweets; also the officers and men of the Special Boat Section who trained and took passage with us on these operations; and, of course, not least our passengers and, for one patrol, our United States Navy Commanding Officer.

Of the officers and men of the *Seraph* I would like to think, and I am sure they would too, that by their actions and be-haviour, when of necessity they were living in such close contact with our guests aboard, they gave a better understand-ing of the British Character and way of life. I hope that they are as proud of having served with me as I am of having served with them.

In my present appointment, in command of the Third Submarine Squadron, it gives me much pleasure that *Seraph* is one of the submarines in the Squadron. Although outwardly she now looks very different from her profile in the war-time years and she can no longer be aggressive, she still plays a very useful and unique rôle.

N. L. A. JEWELL,
Captain, Royal Navy,
Commander, Third Submarine Squadron.

"*It was, I think, unique in the history of the two nations that a United States naval officer should be placed in nominal command of a British submarine thereby making her the only warship on active service to be commanded by two captains.*"

> Rear-Admiral G. B. H. Fawkes, R.N., Captain of the Eighth Submarine Flotilla during the period covered by this book.

"The Ship with Two Captains *is an appropriate title for a book about* Seraph, *a submarine with a wonderful career. My most vivid recollection of her today is of the time I first boarded her at night. I particularly noticed her small dimensions which did not exactly fit my 6 foot 3 inches. But beyond that I was deeply impressed with the business-like appearance of her crew. They were fine-looking lads with whom I was glad to go most any place.*"

> General Mark Wayne Clark.

PREFACE

NO Elizabethan man-o'-war or frigate of Nelson's day sailed with a more ardent spirit of adventure than those submarines which maintained the offensive against the Axis supply routes throughout the war in North Africa. A "happy few" were these Mediterranean submariners: yet their exploits rank among the most exciting, bizarre and unique of the war at sea.

In 1939, France possessed more submarines than any other nation and, as in the First World War, naval control of the Mediterranean was left to the French Navy. But, when diplomatic relations with Italy worsened, the Admiralty began to divert some of our overworked submariners from the Far East and Indian Ocean to plug any leak which might be sprung due to an Italian declaration of war. One of these, H.M.S. *Olympus*, sailed at eight hours notice from her Eastern base and dashed more than 12,000 miles to the Mediterranean. Her crew, clothed only for the tropics in shorts and sandals, found themselves in high seas and icy gales. The coxswain saved them from freezing to death by sewing trousers from canvas for the entire crew.

When Italy entered the war and France fell, there were only ten British submarines in the Mediterranean and three of these were lost on their first war patrol in the area. Yet from this small beginning grew the force which was to play such a large rôle in sweeping the Germans from Africa and bringing Italy to her knees.

There is no such person as a typical submarine captain. Here and there among them is an inheritor of the Drake tradition whose bearded face and individual habits give colour to his personality, who flavours his deeds and words with a touch of his own character so that they are passed from mouth to mouth until a legend is formed around his name. There are many others who lack such outward characteristics; who would pass unnoticed in a crowd except perhaps for an unusually long row of medal ribbons.

Among these are the legendary names of the Mediterranean theatre—Lieutenant-Commander Malcolm David Wanklyn, V.C., D.S.O., R.N., who sank three enemy U-boats and 90,000 tons of shipping; Commander A. C. C. Miers, V.C., D.S.O., R.N.[1] who stayed inside an enemy harbour for seventeen hours in order to sink two supply ships; Commander J. W. Linton, V.C., D.S.O., R.N., who sank a cruiser, destroyer and U-boat plus 100,000 tons of enemy shipping.

Every now and then the Navy moulds men such as these as examples to future generations. Yet they were of the same basic calibre as all submariners of the Royal Navy, unassuming, specially qualified, intensively trained and peculiarly fitted to their duties. During the war not all submariners were volunteers, but it was rare for anyone to request a transfer back to General Service in surface ships.

On one Mediterranean patrol a submarine was under heavy depth charge attack; the batteries were leaking, lights had failed and the depth gauge smashed. In his report of the action, the Commanding Officer wrote:

"At that moment when I was uncertain whether I was on the bottom or not—and felt more than a little worried—I was handed a chit on which was written: 'Able Seaman John Jones requests to go back to General Service.' "

The submarines of the Mediterranean flotillas rarely saw daylight from the moment they left harbour to the day they returned; for them night and day changed places. They prowled submerged by day on the power of their electric batteries. The men on watch maintained a constant listening watch on the Asdic; occasionally the periscope would be raised to search sea and sky for the enemy. Men off watch kept as still as possible to conserve air which could not be changed until they surfaced after dark. Some slept—sleep came easily in the close atmosphere of a submerged submarine—while others read or played games. These hours of tedium would be shattered by an abrupt call to action followed by periods of great tension.

Then, after dark, the submarine began her day. The diesel engines took over from the batteries and instead of silence there came the throb of engines and the sound of the sea.

[1] Now Rear-Admiral Miers; Wanklyn and Linton were awarded their V.Cs. posthumously.

The boat would lurch and roll and men could breathe easily and move freely. Smokers could light up and cooks would start breakfast. The next meals would be dinner at midnight and supper shortly before dawn.

On the conning-tower bridge an officer and two look-outs constantly raked the darkness for a blacked-out ship, a floating mine or a light ashore. Near at hand alarm bells waited to summon the crew to diving stations. In this event, the last man down the conning-tower hatch would shut the "lid" and the submarine would dive. The term "crash dive" meant nothing to submariners then; every dive was a crash dive.

Inside, the remainder of the crew carried out their "daily" chores. Tightly packed, with a bewildering mass of instruments and machinery demanding constant attention, there was plenty to do during the hours on the surface.

Such was the normal routine established by the "happy few" until August, 1942, when a newcomer to this theatre of operations spoiled the pattern and, refusing to be regimented into stereotyped patrols, set off on a series of eccentric and unique adventures. These soon earned for her a reputation for unpredictable antics. In the more sensational Press she became the "Secret Mission Submarine"; her cynical sisters christened her "Ferdinand" after the famous bull who preferred chewing such delicacies as buttercups and daisies to eating dirt in the bullring.

This was the newly-built P.219 who sailed in childlike innocence under the name *Seraph*: it was her fate to punctuate normal patrols with secret operations which were to help change the destinies of nations—no idle claim, this.

Seraph's most cherished "line" is not concerned with the destinies of nations but with strange behaviour in her chain of command. For, not satisfied with one commanding officer and one flag, *Seraph* acquired two captains and two flags. In both cases the additions to her complement were American— and in no time at all she answered only to orders given in a curious Anglo-American mixture soon dubbed "Seraphese".

Sometimes she preferred the Stars and Stripes to the White Ensign but always played strictly fair with the nations they represented. On one trip the United States captain had to be content to sail in H.M.S. *Seraph*, on another the British commander imperturbably accepted the fact that his ship had become the U.S.S. *Seraph*. It was Seraphese or nothing under these circumstances.

Representing the growing might of America in this ship with two captains was Captain Jerauld Wright, U.S.N. He had never before served in a submarine and cheerfully admitted that if, by any miracle, he could persuade *Seraph* to submerge he was "damn sure I'd never get her to come up again". The Royal Navy's contribution to the command was Lieutenant Norman Limbury Auchinleck Jewell, R.N., who had always served in submarines but had to keep a wary eye on his partner's four gold rings.

Any other submarine but *Seraph* might have found this something more than a mere tricky situation, but the ship with the face of a benevolent bull painted on her conning tower took it in her stride and leapt joyously into the Mediterranean war to carry out some of the most bizarre "political operations" in naval history.

Her crew of forty-four lived in danger for eighteen months. Under the grinding tension of operating silently in unknown enemy waters, a cough sounded like a thunder-clap; while the almost inaudible thud of driftwood against her side jarred threadbare nerves like the explosion of a torpedo.

They were sailors and some of these hazards were abnormal to their training. There was no escaping the tension even in harbour, for the end of one mission meant only more nervous anticipation of the next. Rarely, if ever, did they know the full importance of what they were doing—only the stomach-sinking orders which sent them into enemy waters to use not their guns, but their wits.

Without the safety valve of orthodox action with guns and torpedoes they lived in constant fear of noise, of darkness, of sleep. Friendships broke apart suddenly and easily; laughter came too quickly and too loudly; uneasiness became the normal, while relaxation proved impossible.

Above everything else was the child-like dependence of all on their one link with safety—*Seraph*. If she appeared depressed or behaved sluggishly, then the crew worked frantically to find the cause. When she leapt buoyantly at every change of speed or helm the crew were confident of success. And round the clock

they devoted their time almost passionately to ensuring that
Seraph suffered no hidden ills which might one day sever their
only escape line from danger.

This is *Seraph*'s story. Many people have given of their time
generously to assist me in gathering material; perhaps I will be
forgiven if I leave them anonymous and express my deepest
appreciation. I must, however, offer particular thanks to those
senior and honorary seraphim, both past and present, who have
given me ready help and advice, notably:
Admiral Jerauld Wright, U.S.N., now Commander-in-Chief
of the United States Atlantic Fleet and Supreme Allied
Commander (Atlantic); Capt. N. L. A. "Bill" Jewell, R.N.,
now Captain (S/M) 3 at Rothesay; Rear-Admiral G. B. H.
"Barney" Fawkes, R.N., recently retired Flag Officer in
Command Submarines; Rear-Admiral N. V. Dickinson, R.N.
(Retd), former head of the Advance Landings Force; Brigadier
Bradley Gaylord, formerly of the United States Army Air
Force, who gave me permission to quote from his diary;
Lieutenant-Commander J. A. "Sus" Spender and Commander
David Scott, formerly First Lieutenants of the *Seraph*; Chief
Petty Officers Hinds and Wiseman, two former seraphim still in
daily contact with her; Lieutenant H. M. Ellis, present captain
of *Seraph* and his officers for allowing me to visit her during
the preparation of this book; the Ziff-Davis Co. for per-
mission to quote from their wartime publication "Secret
Service Submarine".

B

CHAPTER ONE

WHALE OF A TIME

SERAPH was born on May 27th, 1942—a slender girl, darkly-painted and freshly scrubbed of the coal dust and dirt of Barrow shipyard. She was the medium-sized child—some 217 feet long and weighing 715 tons—of a destroyer also named *Seraph* who had lived for only sixteen years before being broken up in 1934.

On this spring day the forty-four seraphim who made up her crew commanded by Lieutenant N. L. A. Jewell—known since joining submarines as "Bill"—took her to sea, slapped her bottom and began the trials which would shake down her birth pains. They were well satisfied. She maintained a top surface speed of 14 knots, and 9 when dived; her first sounds from the 3-inch guns on the foredeck and the six torpedo tubes in her bows were those of an angry adult rather than a child.

Later that day Jewell signed the official receipt on behalf of Their Lordships of the Admiralty and took possession from Vickers-Armstrongs, the builders, of the most deadly instrument of war of its size yet devised by an offensive-minded Navy. Drinks were poured in the tiny Wardroom and the ship's officers joined with dockyard officials in toasts to the success of this newest addition to the submarine fleet.

In the afternoon, Jewell mustered the crew ashore, gave his Commissioning Speech and signalled the Admiralty that he was ready to start working up—that period of a submarine's life when she travels from babyhood through childhood to teen-age youthfulness in a matter of weeks. The crew try to iron out all her faults and co-ordinate their forty-four individual characteristics into one fast-thinking team.

Norman Limbury Auchinleck Jewell, twenty-eight years old and a cousin of the famous Field Marshal, was already a veteran of the submarine war. More than 6 feet tall and as slimly rakish as his *Seraph*, he was, like many submariners and fighter pilots, almost incongruously large for the confined

quarters in which he had chosen to devote his professional life.
Endowed with a disarming charm, wit and a quick smile
it would be difficult to imagine anyone more suited to lead his
crew.

He had been First Lieutenant of the submarine *Truant*
commanded by Lieutenant-Commander H. A. V. Haggard
in November, 1940, when she was sent to patrol off the heavily
mined coast east of Tripoli. Haggard had been told not to
approach within fifteen miles of the shore. But after several
days with nothing but the tedious activities of an Italian minesweeper to watch through the periscope, he decided to penetrate
the minefield by following in the wake of the Italian and charting the swept channel.

Bill Jewell was one of the few aboard who did not regard
his captain as a raving lunatic. They followed the minesweeper
to within seven miles of Tripoli before turning back; and
when they returned to base Haggard was saved from a court-
martial for disobeying orders by handing the Commander-in-
Chief, Mediterranean, a safe passage through the minefield
should a landing or bombardment of Tripoli be contemplated.
Jewell learned then that daring is condoned by senior officers
only if it is coupled with reasonable caution—and succeeds.[1]

In August, 1940, Jewell was still Haggard's Number One
when *Truant* surfaced in the Bay of Biscay to intercept a ship
bound for Bordeaux. It was the Norwegian steamer *Tropic Star*
which had been captured recently by the German armed
raider *Orion*. She was sailing under a prize crew while the
Norwegian sailors were imprisoned below with the crew of the
British ship *Haxby* which had been sunk by the *Orion* and her
crew sent aboard *Tropic Star* to be taken to Germany into
captivity.

As *Truant* approached and fired a shot across her bows, the
Germans laid scuttling charges, released the prisoners and
abandoned ship. *Truant* was able to pick up the Master and
twenty-two survivors of the *Haxby* and the Norwegian captain
and his wife. The German prize crew were left in the lifeboats
after Haggard warned their skipper that he was responsible for

---

[1] Haggard's "disobedience" was rewarded in April, 1941, when he led
battleships of the Mediterranean Fleet through the minefield to bombard
Tripoli.

the fate of his own men. In any event, Jewell had reported that the *Truant* would hold no more extra passengers.

There is little doubt that *Truant* paved the way for Jewell's future successes. By the time he left her the Commander-in-Chief, Mediterranean, had reported: "The operations of *Truant* have been a model of daring and enterprise tempered with just the right degree of caution."

For the next few weeks, *Seraph* underwent a severe training course at Holy Loch on the Clyde. Day after day she dived, surfaced, dived, evaded destroyer hunters and navigated through dummy minefields. During this period Jewell was able to test the reliability of his officers.

Darkly handsome, fun-loving John Antony Spender, his First Lieutenant, known to all submariners as "Sus" Spender, proved capable of handling both ship and crew immaculately. He could not fault Lieutenants Edsell and Norris, navigator and watchkeeper respectively; Lieutenant Bolton, the short, slight Gunnery and Torpedo Officer thought of little else but his guns and torpedoes even when sleeping; and the Warrant Engineer, Mr. R. J. Sutton, could be relied upon to keep the engines running sweetly. The average age of the six was twenty-four.

Most tiresome of their training antics were the continuous exercises with a Commando unit of three capricious young Army officers—Captain Godfrey B. Courtney, who answered promptly to the nickname "Jumbo" because his size and weight were almost unbelievable in one of such tender age; Captain R. P. Livingstone, whose studious looks belied a terrifying addiction to navigation and throat-slitting; and Lieutenant J. P. Foote, a smooth-faced infant of twenty whose greatest wish was to fire two tommy guns at the same time in lone battle.

These three practised embarking and disembarking from *Seraph* in small canvas-covered canoes called folbots in any sort of weather until the interest of the crew turned to boredom when the Commandos became so good that there were no more spills.

They were able to bid farewell to their Commando friends on July 15th, 1942, when they sailed for Norwegian waters to carry out their first operational patrol.

The North Sea was cold and choppy despite the sun which

shone overhead. But *Seraph*, like the frolicsome colt she was, flexed her muscles by bucking on the surface and settled down to a steady gait only when submerged.

Jewell and his officers hoped they might sight the German battleships, *Scharnhorst* and *Gneisenau*, both known to be operating in these waters. Almost every other ship in the Royal Navy had met this elusive pair at some time or other, but it was not to be *Seraph*'s fortune on this trip.

Instead, shortly after dark on July 24th, when she had just finished shaking off the water after surfacing, they sighted an enemy U-boat trimmed down on the surface little more than half a mile away. The conning tower crew fell down into the control room as Jewell gave orders to dive and Spender trimmed her neatly at periscope depth. The attack team closed up in the control room—"Sus" Spender muttering orders softly to the coxswain and a rating at the bright metal wheels which operated the fore and after hydroplanes controlling the trim of the ship; Edsell, the navigator at his chart and plot, known as the "fruit machine", because when estimates of the enemy's course and speed were fed into it the robot calculated how far ahead of the target the torpedoes should be fired; the Engine Room Artificer at the air vents which controlled the submarine's depth; the quartermaster at the wheel; and the stoker who stood by to raise and lower the periscope at Jewell's command.

Jewell himself stood in the centre, hunched at the sights. There could be no doubt it was the enemy; no other Allied submarines were in the area. A hush fell upon the crew. Suddenly Jewell rapped out his orders.

"Stand by to fire Number One tube."

"Fire Number One."

Bolton pulled the firing lever, a light flashed above him and the torpedo hurtled out—*Seraph*'s first shot fired in anger.

A slight shock ran through the submarine followed by moments of suspense. Then came the muffled crash of an explosion which shook her from stem to stern. Forty-four smug smiles appeared on the faces of the crew. They had scored a hit. In a few minutes now they would hear the death agonies of the sinking U-boat as it was crushed by the pressure of water.

Minutes ticked by and still there was only silence. Puzzled looks replaced the grins. Jewell gave the order to go up and the conning tower crew dashed to the bridge as the submarine broke surface. Anxious eyes scanned the darkness; there was nothing in sight.

Gradually premonition of the truth grew in Jewell's eyes. The target had shown every characteristic of an enemy U-boat; it had travelled across their bows on a steady course at slow speed and at first sight had seemed to be a U-boat, but . . . *Seraph* continued her patrol.

The truth emerged a few days later. A sister submarine reported sighting a dead and badly-damaged whale floating on the surface. *Seraph* blushed while her crew sought what glum satisfaction they could from the thought that at least they could hit what they aimed at, carefully ignoring the obvious fact that whales are not trained to take avoiding action.

When they returned to the Clyde base of Rothesay and Jewell handed in his report of the patrol to the flotilla captain it was not long before the story flashed from Scapa Flow to Whitehall that *Seraph* had successfully completed a whaling trip to northern waters.

She sailed to war seriously on August 12th to join the Eighth Submarine Flotilla at Gibraltar. Slipping from Holy Loch in the early morning, she parted company with her destroyer escort in the Irish Sea. Under a bright and cloudy sky and helped along by a stiff westerly breeze she left England behind and began her crossing of the Bay of Biscay, surfaced by night and submerged by day. The first few days were uneventful, a Hudson aircraft being sighted on the 15th and a few fishermen passed them by two days later.

On the 19th, while surfaced in the afternoon in a total bombing restriction area—an area in which aircraft were forbidden to bomb because any submarines sighted there would be allied ships either on passage or patrol—they spotted what looked like a Hudson gliding out of the sun with engines stopped. To Jewell this was ominous; he sounded "Diving Stations" on the klaxon alarm hooter and the conning-tower crew dropped through the hatch into the control room. Jewell, last man down, had just slammed the "lid" when the first bombs fell around them.

Seraph shuddered under the impact of the shock and went down deep. Three more bombs dropped, further away this time, and she stayed down for another hour before Jewell thought it safe to assume that the attacker had left in search of easier prey.

The rest of the voyage was uneventful and, on the 25th, *Seraph* was escorted into Gibraltar to tie up alongside the Eighth Flotilla's depot and parent ship, H.M.S. *Maidstone*. When Jewell handed in his report of the air attack to Captain Barney Fawkes, or Captain (S/M)8, as he was officially referred to, signals began to fly between the Rock and Whitehall. Jewell was convinced he had been attacked by a Hudson in an area where bombing was forbidden. Captain Fawkes wanted an explanation and, when they saw the signalled report, so did Their Lordships at the Admiralty.

Coastal Command denied all knowledge of the attack but an Air Ministry probe produced this rather facetious reply:

"The only aircraft in the vicinity of the attack at the time stated was Whitley bomber 'X' of Number 10 squadron, Bomber Command Officers Training Unit. The pilot has reported attacking a U-boat at that time. He dropped four bombs from 150 feet on what he took to be U-07 or 17. It is submitted that a Whitley aircraft should not be mistaken for a Hudson on a clear day." The numbers referred to were poor identification of *Seraph*'s fleet number, P.219, painted on her conning tower.

This attempt by the R.A.F. to counter-attack the Admiralty brought a curt reply from the Flag Officer in Command of the Submarine Service.

"Submarines waste no time in establishing the exact type of aircraft in sight. In this case the aircraft was gliding out of the sun and it was cool thinking for it to have been identified as even British. Whether the aircraft was a Whitley or a Hudson, whether the submarine was experienced or not, there was absolutely no justification for an attack being made on any submarine in a total bombing restriction area."

Two further incidents reminded *Seraph* that she was on the fringe of the battlefield—an enemy aircraft put several cannon shells through her conning tower and on surfacing near a British merchant ship she was immediately fired at by the excited, over-anxious amateur gunners.

At this time in London, General Dwight Eisenhower, then almost unknown to the British public, had been appointed Allied Supreme Commander of "Torch", code name for the North African invasion. With his deputy, General Mark Clark, Eisenhower set up a planning headquarters at London's Norfolk House where it was quickly decided that the landing points which offered the best strategic objectives were Casablanca, Oran and Algiers. Casablanca was to be an entirely United States operation with an invasion force shipped from America under the command of General George Patton. The combined Anglo-American Army from the United Kingdom would tackle Algiers and Oran, but the first requirement of the planners was a thorough reconnaissance of the beaches and their exits into the hinterland.

Eisenhower arranged with Combined Operations for specially trained Combined Operations Pilotage Parties—COPPs for short—to carry out a beach reconnaissance south of Algiers working from submarines of the Eighth Flotilla at Gibraltar.

The details he passed on to Combined Operations gave little indication of the size, scale and scope of the proposed landings. Owing to this misunderstanding the preliminary reconnaissance operations were whittled down to one COPP party in one submarine. At Gibraltar Captain Fawkes was asked to provide that submarine; because she was new to the Mediterranean and had been in harbour for more than a week, he chose *Seraph*.

It was first necessary for her to acquire operational experience in the theatre, for the Mediterranean was one of the most dangerous areas in the world for submarines. "My invariable rule," Captain Fawkes recalls, "was that when a submarine joined the Flotilla she should do one or two runs on the 'nursery slopes'—that is do a couple of patrols where enemy activity was slight. This gave her the feel of Med. conditions." The calm, blue water was so transparent that an aircraft could spot a submerged submarine with comparative ease. This could have been offset by building submarines which could dive deeper but for the numerous coastal shallows in which they were forced to operate, and the Italian habit of sailing their convoys close to the shorelines.

In such circumstances, the submarines carried out attacks in water which was too shallow to help them avoid counter-attacks and made them clearly visible from the air.

There were also too many brilliantly sunny days when the sea was as smooth as a sheet of window glass. A periscope poked up under these conditions left a tell-tale feather of foam which could be seen for miles by aircraft or surface ships. And when the calm gave way to storm and the seas began to boil, the submarines could find little tranquillity submerged in their shallow patrol areas where the disturbance often spread downwards to the seabed. It was then that life really became arduous for the submariner.

Over and above all these hazards, the Italian Navy had taken considerable pains to lay liberal sprinklings of mines across every channel, alongside coastal convoy routes and out to sea from potential landing points. However, this would be valuable experience.

Some of the crew had served in the Mediterranean before, including Jewell. They were now to learn all over again, this time as a team. Jewell knew already that the old hands of Malta, Gibraltar and Alexandria had by trial and error worked out a set of rules for the game of seeking the enemy. He intended to keep his *Seraph* intact by sticking to the rules as far as possible. It was, for instance, a cardinal and fatal mistake to enter a minefield at anything but maximum depth at which one stayed until clear of danger. Those who attempted to come up even to periscope depth in a minefield rarely lived to report what they saw.

Seraph sailed on September 19th with the COPP party commanded by Lieut.-Commander H. N. C. Willmott. Available space in the for'ard torpedo room was filled with folbots and weapons for Willmott's men to take ashore when recon-noitring the beaches.

While on passage, Jewell learned the reason for the trip. Rumours of a North African invasion had been circulating round the Rock for weeks, but no one knew where, when or how the operation was to take place; not even Willmott. It was, however, common knowledge that it would be no easy task. Vichy France maintained an army of more than 150,000 men in North Africa while they were known to have at least 500 fighter aircraft which, if not modern, were at least superior to the Allied carrier-borne aircraft on which the troops would have to rely for initial cover.

Seraph's officers discussed these and other problems of invasion with Willmott, while on the messdecks, "galley" gossip ran rife. This was the first of her secret missions and the sailors found that for the first time their captain could not tell them the object of the trip. From the moment he had joined as commanding officer, Jewell had decided to keep his men informed of the purpose of every voyage. Now he found this was forbidden on the sensible assumption that if the ship should be sunk and her crew taken prisoner, the less they knew the better. To the seraphim, however, it meant sailing blind, and tension increased as they moved towards the Algerian coast.

The approach lasted nearly a day at a submerged speed of two knots. No one could say if a minefield had been laid off Algiers or not. It was for *Seraph* to find that out and still live to tell the planners of "Torch" in Grosvenor Square. There was no need for Jewell to announce the danger to the crew; they knew it instinctively.

Gently, *Seraph* nudged her way shorewards at periscope depth waiting for the first slight jarring which would tell them they had struck a mine mooring wire. Then it would clatter down the side and they would have to wait while she broke clear; if she didn't, the mine would be pulled down to hit them.

She made it to within three miles of the shore before turning parallel to the coast. Jewell handed over the periscope to Willmott who began taking pictures of the beaches and hills behind them with the automatic camera attached to the periscope lens.

They kept up this procedure for two weeks, taking photographs and drawing outlines through the periscope by day while, at night, *Seraph* went right inshore to launch the folbots and disembark the COPP party who had to land on the beaches and report on the positions of underwater defences, land minefields on the beaches, the state of the terrain and what sort of roads, valleys and hills provided an exit inland from over-crowded beach-heads.

To the crew it was unnatural, nerve-racking work carried on close to shore patrols and gun emplacements. They looked with admiration on the COPP men who concentrated wholly on the job of listing enough information to provide Eisenhower and the leaders of the invasion forces with as complete a picture of the area as possible.

When the job was done, *Seraph* thankfully pointed her nose seawards and withdrew. The return voyage to Gibraltar proved uneventful and the submarine slithered slowly into her berth alongside *Maidstone* at dawn on October 12th.

That same morning Willmott's reports were flown to London where Norfolk House reconstructed the beaches of Algiers and made the first decisions which were to send nearly 100,000 men ashore on soil about which they knew only what had been gathered by *Seraph*.

The crew were a sadder crowd after that trip, but wiser too. They knew more about the North African coast than any other submarine in the Mediterranean and this knowledge and newly-gained experience was to pave the way for their next and even stranger mission.

CHAPTER TWO

OPERATION FLAGPOLE

THIS was Rommel's triumphant hour. His troops were pouring towards Egypt. Reports of a possible Allied invasion at Casablanca and Dakar had reached Berlin, and 100,000 German troops manned the borders of Tunisia ready to march into French North Africa if the Vichy forces failed to throw back the landings. Hitler warned Marshal Pétain that Germany would occupy Vichy France if there was any attempt by the French North Africa forces to defect to the Allies.

Meanwhile, the problem of avoiding a savage encounter with these forces occupied the minds of all connected with "Torch" planning in London. The French administrative machine made it impossible for any one senior officer or politician in the area to be approached. Algeria, Morocco and Tunisia were separate political entities; French West Africa was ruled by Governor-General Pierre Boisson, under direct orders from Metropolitan France.

One great advantage remained. The United States maintained diplomatic relations with Vichy France, and not only did this provide her Ambassador, Admiral William D. Leahy, with opportunities to apply pressure on Marshal Pétain, but also gave the American political representative in North Africa freedom of movement. He was Robert Murphy, ostensibly Counsellor of the American Embassy in Algiers, but in fact chief of a "Special Missions" team.

Under an agreement with General Weygand, the personal representative of Pétain in North Africa, the United States was permitted to ship essential civilian supplies into the area. In order to ensure that these did not fall into enemy hands, Murphy insisted on having twelve American "control officers" to superintend distribution. Weygand consented and a round dozen civilians arrived from America to work under Murphy. Each was a trained secret service agent specially selected for the mission.

But even this intelligence network was insufficient for Eisenhower's needs. He wanted a personal report on North Africa, and the chance came early in October, when Murphy was called back to Washington by President Roosevelt. One afternoon during this visit, Murphy walked into the office of General Marshall, Commander-in-Chief of the United States Army, carrying a briefcase.

Ten minutes later he emerged through the back door equipped with papers identifying him as Lieutenant-Colonel Herbert McGowan of the United States Army. He was taken by car to an airfield and some hours later met in Scotland by Colonel Julius Holmes, political adviser to the "Torch" planners in London.

At Norfolk House he gave Eisenhower a personal report: but even this was outdated, for on his return to Algiers— after reverting to his own identity—he was approached by French underground leaders with a proposal that he should meet privately with the commander of the Algiers garrison, General Charles Mast.

As a result of this secret conference, Murphy was able to send a cable to Eisenhower saying that General Mast and other leaders of the French community in North Africa wanted an American delegation to meet them at a secret rendezvous near Algiers. The purpose was to discuss co-operation instead of resistance when the Allies launched their invasion. The rendezvous was to be a lonely house on the shore sixty miles west of Algiers. The delegation would travel in an American submarine and include an officer of general's rank.

This message reached London on October 17th, and the date set for the rendezvous was four days ahead. General Mark Clark, the Deputy Allied Commander for "Torch", offered his services at once as the only available person of general's rank. This was agreed by Eisenhower and the same night the two American officers went to No. 10 Downing St., where they met the Prime Minister, Lord Mountbatten, Sir Dudley Pound and Anthony Eden.

The proposed mission was given immediate approval by Churchill, who rose to the occasion with his customary grandeur:

"The entire resources of the British Commonwealth are at your disposal. I want to assure you at once how important it will be to get all necessary information and cut down French resistance. It will save countless numbers of British and American lives."

It was mainly for this reason that the mission was to be attempted. In all, some 150,000 British and American soldiers would be poured on to the beaches on D-Day. If the French would let them through without resistance there was no saying how many lives would be saved. With Churchill's approval there could be no more delay.

Included in Clark's team were Brigadier-General Lyman "Lem" Lemnitzer, head of the Allied Forces Plans Section; Colonel Arch Hamblen, shipping and supply expert for "Torch"; Colonel Julius C. Holmes, former State Department officer; and tall, lean Captain Jerauld Wright, U.S. Navy, Eisenhower's naval liaison officer.

General Spaatz, commander of the American Air Force in Britain, was contacted and asked to provide two Flying Fortress bombers to take off that night. A car had arrived at Grosvenor Square to take the delegation to the airfield, and Clark was about to take his leave of Eisenhower when the red "Secret" telephone on the Supreme Commander's desk rang urgently. It was the Prime Minister.

"Has Clark got civvies?" he snapped.

"I don't think so, sir," replied Eisenhower.

"Well, tell him to take some, then" said Churchill. "Never know when he might need them. Things might go wrong."

A frantic scramble began as the Americans turned Headquarters upside down and grabbed suits of clothes from those of the staff who had been unfortunate enough to keep a change of clothing in their offices. Finally, General Clark decided it would be better if the mission wore uniform.

Weather delayed take-off until the following morning and the time was used in packing a considerable quantity of equipment into as small a space as possible. A hurried search of London banks by anxious staff officers who uprooted managers from their beds in faraway places produced $1,000 in Canadian five- and ten-dollar gold pieces, a further 1,000 in American currency and a few *Napoleon d'or*.[1] This was divided among the five officers and strapped round their waists in money belts. It would be useful should they have to try and bribe their way out of French hands.

The weather did not clear sufficiently until dusk on the 18th, when they drove to Polebrook, seventy miles northwest of London, but it grew worse again before they arrived. The next morning, Washington joined the game by signalling: "Agree [code name for Mark Clark] is to proceed at once with his mission." As Clark had been trying to get away for twenty-four hours, the five officers exchanged sour smiles.

Only two clear days were left for the rendezvous by the time they eventually took off at dawn on the 19th, with the leading plane piloted by Major Tibbets, U.S.A.A.F., who much later in the war was to drop the atom bomb on Hiroshima.

The two planes landed safely at Gibraltar in the afternoon and the five officers were whisked to Government House, residence of the Governor-General, Lieutenant-General Sir Frank Noel Mason-MacFarlane.

Meanwhile, in *Seraph*, lying alongside *Maidstone*, the quiet of harbour routine was shattered by a signal from the Admiralty to Captain Fawkes:

"*Seraph is allocated to special political operations from this date. Utmost discretion in briefing of officers is necessary and all further orders are to be destroyed after committal to memory.*"

Now there was hustle and bustle where a moment before there had been an ordinary, normal day. Captain Fawkes sent for Jewell and told him to prepare to receive a Commando unit and several V.I.P.s. *Seraph* was to be ready for sea at immediate notice.

In the afternoon two cars drew up on the jetty alongside *Maidstone* and three Commandos went aboard, crossed her decks and looked down upon *Seraph*. "Sus" Spender, talking to Leading Stoker Hinds on the bridge, glanced up indignantly as a joyous "Oi, you" reached him from above. Then he grinned and sent Hinds below for Jewell who came up to see the huge form of Jumbo Courtney galloping lightly down

[1] Each of the party was given a *Napoleon d'or* after the mission by Mark Clark. When they meet today he who cannot produce his piece buys the drinks.

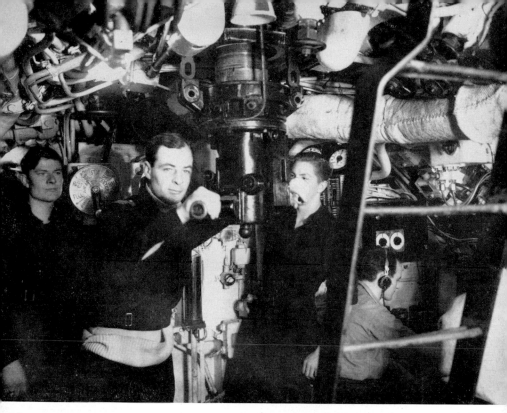

Lieutenant Jewell at the periscope on *Seraph*'s return from landing secret agents in enemy territory.

Seraph at Chatham after a year's service in the Mediterranean.

Twelve men of *Seraph*'s crew playing crib in a space no bigger than the average cupboard ashore.

the swaying gangway. Behind him were the smiling shapes of Livingstone and Foote—their old Commando friends from the training days in Scotland.

In their wake came four folbots, oars, tommy-guns and supplies. When these had been stowed forward, the Commandos went below to speculate on what was afoot. They knew as little as Bill Jewell and his officers.

The sight of the soldiers had started rumours flowing through the messdecks and a steady stream of sailors began to linger near the Wardroom. The "buzzes" that day were wide of the mark. By nightfall the sum knowledge of what lay ahead for *Seraph* was that "somebody" had to be landed "somewhere".

Later in the evening a messenger arrived from *Maidstone* with a request that Jewell report to Fawkes immediately. He found the Captain waiting for him on *Maidstone*'s quarterdeck. Fawkes beckoned him to follow as he crossed the gangway ashore to a waiting car. As it left the dockyard, Fawkes told him that an important Anglo-American conference was about to be held at Government House and he thought it advisable for Jewell to be there. He would say no more.

The mystery deepened when they were ushered into a room dazzling with gold braid. In addition to the Governor-General, Jewell recognised Admiral Sir Frederick Edward Collins, commanding the North Atlantic Station, and with a sense of shock recalled newspaper pictures he had seen of General Mark Clark, the six foot plus Deputy Supreme Allied Commander.

"He looked serious and thoughtful," Jewell said later, "and opened the proceedings by giving us briefly the facts that had led him to come to the Rock. Then he announced gravely that he wanted to proceed to a certain point on the North African coast to rendezvous with some French officials. Anyone looking at me then—and I was standing well in the background —would have seen the slight start that ran through me at this news. Now I knew where *Seraph* came in and I felt both excited and flattered and thankful that we had been selected for the job.

"General Clark continued by giving us a clear picture of the political scene and why he wanted the British element played

c

down and the American influence to be always in the foreground. He then asked if our submarine could get him there by the 21st or 22nd at the latest. We were to be 'American'."

At this stage of the conference, General Clark's records show that he was feeling "less certain of the success of the mission" than ever before. He says he needed support, but "got little encouragement". The Navy people were taking rather a dim view of this whole mad American adventure. They talked of thick shore patrols, plenty of spotting planes and a French Navy and Air Force. "What I needed was someone to say: 'O.K. We'll get you in there and out.' "

Real opposition came from Admiral Collins who had not been briefed beforehand of the reason for Clark's arrival. He considered that it would be madness for a submarine to approach an enemy coast during the full moon to land a shore party—and in the normal course of events he would be right—but this was a secret mission undertaken in abnormal and almost desperate circumstances. And the Admiral needed to be convinced.

The Governor was known to be a stubborn man—in Moscow during the summer he had insisted on wearing traditional British Army tropical shorts although fully aware that the only shorts known to the Russians were underpants—and he remained quiet while the Admiral argued with General Clark and Captain Wright.

Eventually, Clark rose to his feet and stated flatly: "Gentlemen, there is no further use in argument. *We are going.* This trip has been decided by our two Governments and I don't intend to call it off."

He turned to Captain Fawkes: "Do you think," he said slowly, "that in existing weather conditions my party could be landed before the full moon in two or three days' time?"

This placed Fawkes in what might have been a tricky position, but he had liked the look and sound of Clark. Keeping his eyes straight ahead, he replied: "I think we could land you all right, but it may not be before full moon. However, from what I have heard here, your mission is pretty important, so if we just accept all risks, we can land you at any time you like—or try to, anyway."

The grimness unwound from Clark's face. He grinned for the

first time that evening and murmured: "Thank you, Capt. Fawkes, now we are getting somewhere."

Fawkes turned to Bill Jewell.

"I think you ought to meet Lieutenant Jewell, commanding officer of *Seraph*, General Clark. If you go"—he had to say that because the final decision on whether *Seraph* should be risked for this mission rested with the Governor and Admiral Collins —"he will be taking you. He knows that part of the Algerian coast better than anyone here, I think."

Bill was about to salute when his hand was grabbed by Clark's.

"What do you think, son? Can you get us there and back, even during the full moon?"

Taking his cue from Fawkes, Jewell replied: "Of course, sir. No trouble at all if the enemy stays blind and deaf."

"When can you get me there?"

"If we leave tonight, we can make it by the 22nd. That's about the quickest you can count on, sir."

Fawkes intervened to say: "I've had the submarine ready to sail all day. All the necessary landing equipment is aboard and we have recently received a few 'walkie-talkie' radio sets so I sent a couple of those aboard as well. You can go tonight if you like."

Clark grinned at both officers and, with the characteristic informality which seemed to stamp all critical conferences, said: "Thanks." Then he turned to Mason-MacFarlane and Admiral Collins.

"Now, are you going to let me have that submarine and plan the details with me?"

The Governor said: "I think that settles it. If the Navy can get you there and back, we'll go ahead. I'll inform London accordingly."

Now that he had been made aware of the mission's importance, Admiral Collins moved with astonishing speed. He told Barney Fawkes to make out the necessary orders for *Seraph* and set in motion the whole planning apparatus to ensure that *Seraph* and Clark would be in constant communication with the Rock.

General Clark later made a note in his diary: "Apart from Barney Fawkes, the most encouraging person I met on the

Rock was young Norman Limbury Auchinleck Jewell. He bucked me up immensely."

As the conference was about to break up, Fawkes said it would be better if the Americans did not troop aboard *Seraph* "en masse", a procedure which would quickly be picked up by Axis agents and transmitted to Berlin. He suggested that it would be wiser if all concerned dined with him aboard *Maidstone* and then sauntered casually, singly or in pairs, down to *Seraph*.

Jewell had to hurry back to prepare *Seraph* for sea, so he drove away from Government House first. Once outside and away from governors, admirals and generals, he was able to concentrate on the expedition ahead. He could imagine that it might easily become a lively affair from the moment they put to sea until the Americans were returned to the Rock.

He thanked heaven for *Seraph*—his first command and one of the most dependable boats in the Service. It would be a new experience for the little boat but one which, he felt, she would take in her stride. The fate of thousands tied up with "Torch" would hinge on her reliability.

When he reached *Seraph* his officers were waiting in the Wardroom with the three Commandos. The latter were fully prepared for almost anything with sub-machine guns, pistols, knives, signal lamps, walkie-talkie radio sets and a long list of really nasty devices peculiar to their trade.

Jumbo Courtney glanced up hopefully. "What's it all about, Bill ? We know you can tell us the worst."

"Wait and see, chaps. Just wait and see," said Jewell.

Dinner in the privacy of the Captain's cabin aboard *Maidstone* that night was a jovial affair with hardly a mention of North Africa. Jewell described it later: "The Americans were in good spirits, laughing and joking and never revealing a hint of the coming trip. I've rarely seen five men more outwardly untroubled; yet with the possible exception of Captain Wright, none of them knew anything about submarines and much less of the inherent viciousness of collapsible boats in a ground swell or choppy sea. I believe they had reached a decision that General Clark was to voice later—'submarines and small boats were out of their ken and they would leave those problems to me and the Commandos'."

Jewell returned to *Seraph* early to inspect her prior to sailing. He merely told his officers to expect more passengers. Courtney and his two assistants were grouped on the deck below chatting softly. They became suddenly silent as the lighted port of *Maidstone* disgorged two United States Army colonels who came across the gangplank. Jewell led the first guests below and then returned to the bridge to welcome the next. This was Captain Wright. The faces of the Commandos froze except for three pairs of eyes that blinked slowly and incredulously.

A few minutes later the Commandos received their final shock when they saw the star-sprinkled shoulders of two American generals coming aboard and quickly recognised the large figure of General Clark.

Jewell and his officers had no easy task in making their guests comfortable. It is generally understood that no oyster clings more jealously to its shell than the captain of a ship to his quarters. They are sacred to him and restricted to his personal and private use. It was a tradition to which Bill Jewell conformed completely, but here was a different case. His American guests—among them a senior naval officer who had authority to take over command if necessary—were quite unused to the cramped quarters of a submarine. It was possible that for the next few days General Clark in the Mediterranean might mean a lot more to Britain and the United States than even the President and Prime Minister.

He informed the Americans that, for the duration of their stay aboard *Seraph*, they could occupy the Wardroom. The visitors expressed appreciation of the offer and at once rejected it. Jewell insisted but, before they would agree, he had to take them for'ard to show them where he and his officers would sleep in a small secondary Wardroom. Finally convinced that the ship's officers would not have to sleep in the bilges, they at last agreed to take over the Wardroom.

This was about half the size of a railway compartment and had no door. Meals were served on a table in the middle. Five bunks were ranged round the sides—luckily the right number for the guests—placed in two tiers of two, with one by itself for Jewell. Draw-string curtains after the fashion of an American sleeping car gave some privacy. Jewell's bunk was the only lower with no skull-cracking upper, and for this reason appealed specially to General Clark, whose tremendous height made it dangerous for him to stand up without first casting a weather eye aloft. Already he had bruised his head in several slight encounters with the deckhead.

When everyone had been snugged down for the night, Jewell ordered all hands to harbour stations and, shortly before midnight, *Seraph* slipped from harbour and headed for Africa.

It had been a memorable day and, as he talked with the navigator under the stars, Jewell was well pleased and proud that it was his ship which had been chosen.

"Operation Flagpole", code name for Clark's mission, had begun.

CHAPTER THREE

"SAVE THE OARS"

URING the moonlit passage southwards a normal
bridge personnel of an Officer-of-the-Watch and two
look-outs kept station astern of an escorting destroyer.
At dawn, dimmed signal lamps blinked as the escort bade the
submarine farewell and wished her good hunting. Jewell came
up, dressed in an old pair of grey flannel trousers and long
white, roll-necked pullover—almost traditional dress for submariners in wartime.

There had been no alarms during the night, but now they
were on their own. The sea was calm and lapped lazily down
Seraph's throbbing sides. Jewell reflected momentarily on the
beauty of a Mediterranean dawn. In the east, the sky was
already turning opalescent to blend with the dark blue of the
retreating night. Although loth to leave this colourful serenity,
he gave Spender orders to dive. Their main danger now would
be enemy aircraft which patrolled the area in flocks of fifty or
more at a time.

Seraph went down and Spender crouched low over the eyepieces as the periscope was raised for a few brief seconds. It
would be poked up and down throughout the day but never
for longer than seconds at a time—the feathers of water around
it would be a sure give-away to any aircraft in the vicinity.

Inside, the cook had finished breakfast and the meals were
being served to all hands off watch. He was a good cook by
naval standards and quite undeserving of Lieutenant Edsell's
caustic comment that he was the only chef afloat who could
mutilate porridge. A patient, philosophical chap, he turned out
poached eggs when conditions were favourable and merely
shrugged and scrambled them when it was rough. In action,
he was a member of the gun's crew.

The Americans were up and had already been on a conducted
tour with Edsell as guide. Because of them, breakfast was being
served at such an unorthodox hour and already the air inside
was becoming stuffy. After the meal, most of the crew off watch

turned in while Mark Clark recruited his fellow-soldiers for a game of bridge. Wright joined Jewell and the other officers for a professional discussion on the merits of their respective navies, tactics and strategy. Later, Mr. Sutton the engineer tried to teach the Americans traditional Royal Navy games such as cribbage and "ukkers"—known ashore as ludo; but they finally returned to their favourite pastime, bridge.

Jumbo Courtney began to get a little restive. He wanted to know what the mission was all about and his claim to be brought into the picture was strong since he and his team would have to make plans for a successful landing. He waited until General Clark was "dummy" and then ventured to ask if he might be briefed on the party's intentions. Clark replied that he would gladly oblige.

The game was interrupted while the three Commandos, Jewell, his officers and the Americans bent cheek to cheek over a large-scale map of the Algiers coast. General Clark pointed at a heavy, pencilled cross.

"That is where we are going. There is a house just there, a large house with white walls and a red-tiled roof. It sits on rather a large hill about halfway between the shore and the coast road. There is a path leading up to it and, down by the beach, a small grove of olive trees where I think we might hide the boats after we land."

Jewell intervened. "That sounds like all Algerian coastal scenery, sir. The whole country is filled with white houses with red-tiled roofs."

"We'll know this one when we see it," replied Clark confidently. "There's a sugar-loaf hill to the left of the house looking from the sea and a small *wadi* that empties into the sea just below it. The people in the house will have a powerful white light shining seaward only. Some of them will be on the beach to meet us."

"Is there any arrangement by which we shall be able to identify the reception party before we land, sir?" questioned Courtney, showing a proper regard for the safety of the party who would be in his care once they left the submarine.

"No, we will have to chance it," Clark replied with a faint smile. "We may walk into a trap. My job lies up in that house and it is no business of mine what happens on the way there or back." His smile widened at the serious expressions on the faces of the three young soldiers. "That's your baby, boys— we are in your hands."

On that note the session ended. The Americans rolled up the map and returned to their cards. Jewell went to join Edsell in the control room and on the way stumbled over a tubular canvas bag filled with something hard. As he cursed, General Lemnitzer looked up from the bridge table.

"That's my bag. I put our money belts in there with a lot of gold, son. We might need it, and anyway the bag is weighted so it won't fall into enemy hands."

Jewell made his way for'ard amused at the thought of *Seraph* becoming suddenly rich. In the control room he ordered the periscope to be raised. Water dripped away from the lens as it broke surface and he saw another typical Mediterranean day— sunny, clear and calm with nothing in sight. He gave routine orders to be called when anything was sighted and left the control room to lie down in the secondary Wardroom.

An hour or two later he was wakened by the sound of laughter and heavy thuds up for'ard. Puzzled, he climbed from his bunk to be greeted by an astonishing scene. The three Commandos had decided the time was ripe for an exercise and had descended on the bridge game. Without waiting politely for the rubber to end—a wise precaution when dealing with very senior officers—they declared firmly that the moment had come for boat drill.

Even Captain Wright was a little shaken at the thought of boat drill in a submerged submarine and shared the astonishment of his four compatriots. Courtney pointed out that there was just enough room between the table and the nearest bulkhead in which to place an open fully-rigged folbot. They would pretend the table was the foredeck of the submarine and practise stepping into the boat.

The Americans had readily agreed to play Courtney's game and watched with interest as he unwrapped the canoe and placed it beside the table. At this stage, Jewell joined the off-duty officers and some ratings who were squeezing as close as possible to watch the exercise.

As Lieutenant Foote was the small boat expert of the three, he took over, and Wright volunteered to be the first victim.

Foote took his arm, helped him to a crouching position on the table and slowly began giving his orders.

"You sit on the edge of the deck, sir—like this. You lower a leg—like this. You place the foot just there and straighten up very carefully, sir. That's right, sir, balance on one leg. That's it. Now the other leg, sir, place it right here and grip with both hands on the side. Now, sir, lower yourself slowly, very slowly —no, no, not like that. . . ." Wright finally completed his exercise and it was General Clark's turn. By this time they had all entered into the fun of the thing and seemed to enjoy being coaxed into doing these strange antics. It soon became clear that Captain Wright was no amateur as a small boat man. This proved a vital piece of news. The five Americans and three Commandos made eight men to be divided between four boats. With a soldier each in three and Captain Wright in another the four United States army officers would have a pair of skilled arms behind them in each boat.

After the drill Spender, now on watch, reported that it was dusk and Jewell gave the order to surface. The quiet hum of the electric motors gave way to the throb of the diesels; a cheering clatter of pots and pans came from the galley and the crew sprang from everywhere ready for breakfast and lighting the cigarettes handed round by Holmes and Hamblen.

On the surface the sea was quiet, the weather good and with every sign of a peaceful night. Jewell stayed on the bridge with the O.O.W. and the two look-outs standing back to back while, down below, the Americans ate a hot meal and once more settled down to their interminable game of bridge. Jewell hoped the Commandos had also bedded down; but it was not to be. A messenger arrived on the bridge with a request from Courtney for permission to come up and speak. No sooner had this been granted than he loomed high on the bridge treading lightly in a pair of rubber-soled moccasins.

"What now, Jumbo?" Jewell asked resignedly.

"Do you think, Bill, you could stop this battleship for a few minutes so that we can have a spot more boat drill? The real thing this time, you know. Makes all the difference, old boy."

For a second Jewell was too shocked to reply. The thought of stopping his ship so that a few passengers could indulge in water sports was rather too much to grasp at first. Then logic prevailed. Courtney was right; a little practice now might save precious minutes when the landing actually took place.

"O.K., Jumbo, but for heaven's sake make it quick."

In a remarkably short time the foredeck became as busy as a film set with the boat expert, Foote, acting as producer. One of the collapsible folbots came up from the fore hatch and was put over the side. Mr. Sutton, the engineer, came up to see why in heaven's name the engines had been stopped. When he saw what was happening he returned below, muttering about soldiers and prophesying disaster just around the corner.

The five members of the cast appeared for the big scene. The bridge was packed tight by this time by duty personnel who blinked at this reversal of all accepted rules for the behaviour of submarines at war.

General Clark, elected as first victim, stuck out a cautious leg towards the pitching canoe and quickly pulled it back again. Foote whispered encouragingly in his ear, but *Seraph* decided to join the game and swung slowly with the wind until she was beam on to the slight swell. This was just enough to give her enough roll to make the foredeck fascinating to watch.

Jewell was none too happy at this prank by his ship and amusement gave way to nervous expectation. He warned his officers and men to keep eyes open for the approach of aircraft and surface vessels. Even this seemed a pointless precaution because he failed to see how he could get the actors below in the event of an alarm. They were obviously enjoying themselves, leaping in and out of the canoes like sprightly cadets.

At last Courtney admitted he was satisfied and magically the folbot and oars vanished down the fore-hatch, and the passengers were back to the Wardroom. Sighing with relief, Jewell saw normal routine return.

At four next morning, the 21st, he was shaken by a messenger who reported a light dead ahead. A few minutes later he could see it in his binoculars. Both Edsell and Spender were on the bridge and now he decided to have Clark and Wright called for a conference.

The two Americans arrived and, while Clark studied the

blurred outline of the coast ahead, Courtney and Livingstone appeared on deck to test their "walkie-talkie" radio sets and the infra-red signal lamps. These lamps showed a light which could not be seen by the naked eye, only through special glasses.

Suddenly, Clark announced softly: "It's a white house, and that light's coming from an upper floor. Yes, there's the sugar-loaf hill to the left! I can just see its outline against the sky. There's a beach below the house and it's got a black splotch on it—that will be the olive grove. Yep, this is the place for us."

He put down his glasses. "You've hit her smack on the nose, Bill. Thanks a lot." Affectionately patting the side of the bridge, he added: "And thanks a lot to you, my girl." *Seraph* rolled with pleasure and came to a stop less than half a mile from the shore.

They wallowed in the swell for a few minutes while Clark, Wright and Jewell discussed the advisability of signalling their presence with infra-red lamps. This was abandoned because dawn was near and similar arrangements had been made for the meeting to take place the following night.

When Clark and Wright had gone below to break the news to the rest of their team, Jewell called the three Commandos to the bridge and gave them an opportunity to study the shore on which they would have to land.

Then, as the first grey signs of dawn appeared in the east, he sent everyone below and told Spender to take *Seraph* down to periscope depth.

At 6.30 a.m. Jewell received a signal from Gibraltar saying that if they did not appear at the rendezvous that night the signal light would be put out at 6 a.m. The reception party would then expect the Americans on each of the next two nights. He made his way to the control room, had the periscope raised and took a look at the house. The signal light was off. He reported this to Clark and arrangements were fixed to make the landing at the first possible moment that night.

The cook had served a meal when Jewell was again summoned to the control room. This time it was because two fishing boats had appeared out of the early morning mist and were laying their trawls within two hundred yards of the ship. This was an unwelcome intrusion and one that might upset the entire scheme. He reported to Clark who took the news casually. The Americans had just finished eating and were back at their bridge game.

"I hope to hell they shove off before we get going," was his only remark. Turning to the Major-General on his right, he said: "I'll double your spades, Lem." For the first time Jewell saw concern on Lemnitzer's face.

If the Americans were not worried, Jewell was. The immense responsibility he carried rested heavily upon him and filtered down through the crew who, not knowing the reason for the mission, had no liking for this penetration of enemy waters and were constantly startled at every jolt or extra heavy bump *Seraph* suffered in fear that she might have struck mines.

Eyes flickered upwards at a report of approaching aircraft. In their tiny living and duty compartments the crew tensed—in this area it must be an enemy and that meant bombs. *Seraph* seemed rigidly expectant—except for that part of her devoted to the game of bridge. Jewell muttered: "Probably a commercial plane."

"Probably", agreed General Clark, still intent on defeating Lemnitzer in spades.

It settled Jewell. His passengers were relying solely upon him while aboard and if they had parked unknowingly in an area which was going to be crowded with fishing boats and aircraft, it was no place for *Seraph*. He gave the necessary orders and, in a few minutes, she was heading out to a patrol line eight miles from the shore. She dived to 80 feet and all hands not on watch turned in.

Jewell would have been even more amazed at the calmness of his guests in the presence of the enemy had he known how heavy was the burden they carried that day; how privately anxious for them were the long hours of waiting. For only they knew that the first assault units for "Torch" had already sailed from the United States under General Patton. If the landing succeeded that night, thousands of troops crossing the Atlantic to take Casablanca would be unopposed; the dreadful alternative of French, British and American soldiers slaughtering each other depended now on *Seraph*, the Commandos and the negotiations in that white house with the red tiled roof.

As the landing party would maintain contact with the

submarine by radio with Courtney handling one "walkie-talkie" and Jewell the other, the two officers planned a form of recognition prefix to their messages. Any deviation from the identification plan would mean that the party had been captured and a French operator certainly trying to lure *Seraph* into a trap.

They found loopholes in each other's suggestions until Jewell produced an old pin-up picture of a lovely film starlet. It was decided that she should become their code—Courtney would prefix his messages by remarking on the upper part of her body and Jewell would reply with counter descriptions of the lower half. Who this young girl was no one can recall; it is deplorable that she will never know what a star rôle she played in this adventure.

In the afternoon, General Clark held another conference to agree what should be done in the event of trouble ashore. Jewell's official report of this says: "It was decided that everyone should land in one flight. Folbots were to close the shore with Holmes and Livingstone in the van to make contact and give the all clear signal. They would flash "K" if all was well, and "F" if there was danger. In the latter event everyone was to return to the submarine, Holmes and Livingstone if they could.

"Once the party was safely ashore they would switch off the light in the house as a signal to me that all was well and that they would return to the beach at the stipulated time. In the event of the party being captured, I was to remain in the vicinity until the 24th and then patrol off a point further westwards until dusk on Monday 25th. If the party could escape they rendezvous with me in an open boat showing a white light by night."

The "stipulated time" for the party's return to the beach was 9 p.m. the next night when Courtney would contact Jewell by "walkie-talkie".

In the casual conversation that followed this decision, both Clark and Wright declared warmly that if "Operation Flagpole" succeeded it would be entirely due to *Seraph*. Jewell thought that was being too generous and preferred to think they meant that it could only be carried out by a submarine. It was agreed that no aircraft or surface ship could have done the job.

Suddenly, Colonel Holmes remembered the civilian suits they had hastily purloined from Norfolk House. He mentioned that they might be useful if the coming conference were suddenly interrupted by the local *gendarmerie* or troops.

"Hell, no," exploded Clark. "We'll go ashore as American officers. It will help if the people ashore are reminded who we are and what we represent."

This reminded him of the three Commandos, and he turned to Courtney.

"You fellows keep in the background as much as possible. I want this to appear an entirely Franco-American affair. With luck they won't recognise your uniforms as British."

This did not seem unlikely. Armed from neck to ankles, they would be hard to distinguish from a trio of cut-throats.

After dark, *Seraph* surfaced to recharge her batteries while Jewell and Clark gazed at the coast from the bridge waiting for the signal light to beam out from the house. Below, the expectant seraphim went to action stations—even the most humble knowing by now that any minute the engines would begin to throb and the most dangerous part of the operation set in motion.

By 10 p.m. Clark showed the first signs of strain. Another half an hour passed before, wearily, he said to Jewell, "I'm going below to get some sleep, Bill. It might be a long wait. Frankly, I don't relish the idea of sweating it out for another day."

Jewell himself was beginning to despair when suddenly shortly after 11 p.m. a thin, pale light gleamed from the house. The signal at last. *Seraph* glided towards the shore, the fore-hatch was opened and the folbots brought out on deck: Courtney, Livingstone and Foote stood by with several of the crew for the disembarkation routine. A messenger was sent to call the Americans while their equipment, including the bag of golden dollars, was stowed into the canoes.

Running almost silently, *Seraph* crept in under the guns of French Algeria. A few minutes before midnight, she stopped only 500 yards from the beach. At a curt, whispered order from Jewell disembarkation began with Livingstone and Holmes in the lead. If it was a trap then Livingstone's tommy-gun would erupt into angry warning.

They got away nimbly and without incident. A minute or two later, Foote and Lemnitzer, carrying the gold and the secret papers, also vanished into the shadows with Hamblen and Wright following closely. That left Courtney and the tall General who carried so much responsibility. The former launched the boat, put one foot in and then—tragedy. The boat capsized and Courtney was "in the drink". Before he could restore order, the boat drifted under the fore plane of the submarine and ominous snappings were heard on the bridge. Eventually he grabbed it and climbed back on board hauling it after him. It was badly damaged.

Without wasting time, he called out to the retreating figures of Hamblen and Wright who fortunately heard and pulled back. Hamblen stepped out, and his place was taken by General Clark, who was taken shorewards by the powerful strokes of Captain Wright. A few minutes later, Courtney and two of the crew had completed hasty repairs to the damaged folbot and Hamblen embarked again when they shoved off, with Courtney pulling so lustily that he managed to overtake Clark and Wright in the surf.

Seraph seemed subdued and quiet as she waited patiently for the signal that all was well. It came an hour later. The light from the house was switched off and Courtney at once called up Jewell on the "walkie-talkie" set.

"She has a lovely pair of breasts, old boy."

"I think her legs are quite nice too," was Jewell's reply.

"Hullo, Jumbo, is everything O.K. ?"

"Fine, Bill. Everybody got ashore safely and the right people were there to meet us."

Then the radio went silent and *Seraph* pointed her nose out to sea. She ran for seven miles, spent the rest of the night charging her batteries on the surface and dived at dawn to sleep and rest before the exertions of the next night.

The strain of crossing into waters filled with the menace of enemy minefields, surface vessels or aircraft had been taking its toll of some of the crew. A bitter quarrel broke out between two former friends—two leading hands, one of whom was married to the other's sister. During the next day the row nearly developed into open battle.

At 8 p.m. *Seraph* surfaced and slowly closed the beach.

A cartoonist's impression of the North African Canoeists Club heading for *Seraph* from the coast.

(*Below*) The members line up to receive decorations for their escapade. *Left to right:* Colonel A. L. Hamblen, Colonel J. C. Holmes, Lieutenant-General Mark Clark, Brigadier-General L. L. Lemnitzer, and Captain Jerauld Wright.

General Mark Clark, Captain Fawkes and Lieutenant Jewell
at a march past of the U.S. Fifth Army in North Africa.

North African invasion forces land on beaches pinpointed by *Seraph*'s trip.

An hour later they were only 600 yards off the beach and
Jewell was waiting for Courtney to come to life on the "walkie-
talkie" set. This long wait for news from ashore had been the
hardest part of the voyage for the crew. Imaginations ran riot
and it was everybody's bet that the shore party had by this
time been shot or captured by some piece of treachery.

At that moment, the Americans led by the Commandos were
scrambling down to the beaches having successfully completed
their negotiations. Parting courtesies had been broken off
hurriedly by the arrival of the police. It seemed that the French
owner of the house had sacked a servant some weeks previously.
The vengeful peasant had got wind of some deep mystery afoot
and had gone to police headquarters and told them it was
weeks since he had seen smoke coming from the chimneys.
"Now look, messieurs, how she belches." The police had
taken the hint.

However, the eight men found themselves on the shore,
but in very different weather from the night before. The
sea was rising and the surf, already rough, was rapidly becoming
impassable for the tiny canvas folbots. *Seraph*, none too happy
at the weather, was nosing in even closer to narrow the gap over
which the shore party must travel.

Meanwhile, Jewell kept calling Jumbo on the "walkie-
talkie". Shortly after 9 p.m. Courtney answered the call.

"Her eyes were rather nice, too."

"So were her ankles. Where the hell have you been, Jumbo?
What's going on?"

"Nothing's wrong but the weather. It's pretty bad in the
surf."

Nevertheless, Courtney tried his luck. He put General
Clark and Livingstone into one canoe and gave it a hard shove
into the surf. A wave caught it, turned it over and tumbled the
unfortunate canoeists into the sea. They waded ashore, pulling
the boat behind them.

They all stripped off their uniforms for the next attempt at
4 a.m. on the 23rd when the weather quietened enough for
another try. Jewell came in to about 300 yards of the shore and
this time Clark decided to send himself and Wright together.
Clothes were rolled up in a bundle and stowed away. Then with
everyone knee-deep in the water they gave the folbot a mighty

D

heave. A seemingly gigantic wave reared up ahead, hovered for a second and crashed down, missing Wright but landing on Clark. Someone shouted: "Save the clothes." To which Wright replied hastily: "To hell with the clothes, save the oars." He carried out his own instruction, grabbed the oars and gave a desperate pull and they were through. The crew gave a soft cheer as the folbot appeared from the darkness and pulled up alongside.

In the starlight Clark appeared in uniform down to his waist but wearing only a clinging pair of white shorts.

The next couple—Lemnitzer and Foote—got away after their boat had capsized at the first attempt and were hustled below with Clark and Wright to be given dry clothes and hot rum. Then the "walkie-talkie" came to life with an urgent appeal from Courtney for *Seraph* to come still closer to the beach. She nudged carefully ahead until she was almost in the surf herself and scraping the bottom. Jewell and his officers held their breath as they saw the headlights of cars streaking down the coast road towards the beach.

Ashore, Colonel Holmes insisted on Courtney and Hamblen braving the water chute next. He hoped that his fluent French might get him out of serious trouble. The pair made it safely to *Seraph* and stayed on deck to see if Holmes and Livingstone could take the plunge before the police cars arrived. They reached *Seraph* with few minutes to spare in the boat which had been damaged the previous night. Jewell called out to his men to drag it aboard, but somehow it eluded them, capsized and sank. *Seraph* turned and raced out to sea in time while astern of her the cars came to a halt on the beach.

The whole operation of embarking the shore party had taken an hour; at 5.40 a.m., when some eight miles out to sea, they dived and headed on a course for Gibraltar. Clark and his team had to be returned speedily and safely to London.

Once dived and the crew back to routine diving stations, Jewell made his way to the Wardroom. There he gave permission for the drink cabinet, normally kept locked at sea, to be opened for all concerned to drink "To the Navy", the traditional toast after the successful completion of a dangerous operation.

Suddenly, Colonel Holmes cut short the merriment with

a question. "Hey, Bill, that last boat which capsized and sank before your boys could bring it inboard—was that mine ?"

"Yes, sir. We didn't have time to rescue it."

"Did you collect its contents ?"

"No, sir. Sorry, but we had to get out of there. We might have stuck on the beach."

"Good God! That boat had my weighted bag with all the papers and money in it."

Laughter vanished at the thought of $2,000 lying a few yards off the beach. However, it was generally agreed that the banks wouldn't miss the odd dollar or two and, in case the bag was by chance washed ashore and found by unauthorised persons, Jewell sent a signal to Gibraltar:

"Agree (code name for Clark) requests you notify Mac-Gowan (code name for Robert Murphy) that the letters he handed Julius (code name for Holmes) were lost when his canoe broke up. They were in weighted bag which may have fallen out. Canoe may float ashore and search of beach should be commenced immediately." In fact, neither canoe nor money was ever found.

Jewell noticed that the three Commandos were missing and found them in the secondary Wardroom having a party. Courtney had written a brief report of what had happened ashore; it shows how simply he disguised the drama of those twenty-four hours.

October 22nd.

0050 Contact made with reception committee.

0125 Folbots concealed in shadow of bushes. Ten minutes later we moved them to house.

1830 Alarm given owing to inquisitiveness of local police who came to investigate activity in house supposed to be empty. Whole party concealed in dusty cellar while local people parleyed with police.

2000 Released from cellar. Personnel and folbots to beach. Sentries posted.

2149 Too rough so returned to house. Fully ready to meet police should they be unfortunate enough to return.

October 23rd

0540 Party re-embarked to submarine. There were enemy

sentries four miles to east of house and two miles to west. I had a look and they had neither boats nor wireless just telephones.

When Jewell handed back the report, Courtney gave him a list of the gear they had been forced to leave behind because of the police. In his own special report of the incident, Jewell lists the missing equipment as including:

3 Thompson sub-machine guns
1 Luger automatic pistol
2 Luger magazines
1 Colt automatic pistol and magazine
1 fighting knife
1 pair of binoculars
15 magazines of machine-gun ammunition
300 rounds of small arms ammunition
2 torches
1 "walkie-talkie" radio set
1 compass

Jewell was surprised. He knew that the three Commandos went into every operation heavily armed. But if they had left this lot ashore and still managed to come back loaded down with knives and arms, they would have been tough customers to meet in a fight on the beach.

Now that he had accounted for the lost equipment a burden seemed to fall from Courtney's shoulders. He expressed his feelings in the Anglo-American new language they were all acquiring and soon to be called "seraphese":

"Bloody glad that goddam operation is over for us, Bill. She's your baby now, buddy. Just see you hit the Rock on the nose. Incidentally it was a damned artistic operation, old boy. No bloodshed at all!"

The following morning Clark decided to hurry matters by signalling Gibraltar for a flying-boat to meet *Seraph* in mid-Mediterranean. Two hours later a big Catalina aircraft appeared and reported ready to pick up passengers.

The weather that afternoon was calm and smooth and, with the air of professionals, the Americans stepped into the three folbots prepared by the Commandos for the trip across to the aircraft which had landed 100 yards away.

The coxswain reported to the bridge and said the crew would like to man the decks to give the Americans a cheer as they left. Jewell gave permission and his men came tumbling up to the decks, still smoking American cigarettes and chewing gum, and gave a full-throated cheer to the departing folbots. Clark, Wright and the rest of the team waved back and the cheering went on until the Catalina had taken off and turned towards Gibraltar.

Jewell was a little puzzled by a cryptic remark made by Clark as he had left the bridge for the last time.

"Thanks for everything, Bill. Don't go away from Gibraltar too soon. I shall have another job for you in a few days."

On his arrival at Gibraltar by Catalina, General Clark and Captain Wright had time to board *Maidstone* and report to Barney Fawkes that all was well with *Seraph*.

Then Clark expressed what he and his team had obviously been thinking and talking about. "You know, Barney, this is the first operation in which any American has had to rely on the co-operation of the three British fighting forces. And, by golly, I'm going to tell Ike that if we have to fight alongside people like yourself, Bill Jewell and the boys of *Seraph* and those Commando cut-throats, then this war is about to be won." This remark did, in fact, set the seal on Anglo-American co-operation, first in North Africa and on to Sicily.

All involved were destined to serve for many long weary months in the Mediterranean theatre and an intimate relationship grew up between *Seraph*, *Maidstone*, Allied Headquarters and later, Clark's Fifth Army headquarters at Ouidja, in Morocco.

Seraph berthed alongside *Maidstone* early on the 25th. She was a little astonished at her welcome; despite the hurried preparation for the invasion evident everywhere on the Rock, congratulatory signals came from all quarters and Captain Fawkes was waiting to board her to address the crew before anyone had a chance to go ashore.

After praising them for a job well done he added: "There is only one thing which might undo all the planning for the North African landings and the purpose of your recent mission—

that is, careless talk when you go ashore. Don't talk to anyone of what you have been doing, not even your mates in *Maidstone* or other submarines which might be in harbour. If anyone wants to know where you went, say it was some cloak-and-dagger stuff you don't know about or that you were on a normal patrol. Anything but the truth or that part of it which you might know about. I could stop leave for a few days, but that would hardly be fair. Instead, have a good time ashore but remember to keep your mouths shut and don't let me down or your commanding officer."

In his personal report to the Commander-in-Chief, Sir Andrew B. Cunningham, known throughout the Navy by his initials "ABC", Fawkes wrote:

"I consider that this operation was carried out in a manner which reflects great credit on Lieutenant Jewell, his ship's company, the Special Service Brigade Section of Combined Operations and, if I may presume to say so, on *Seraph*'s distinguished passengers.

"The latter won the friendship and unbounded admiration of all in the submarine, not least for the manner in which they breasted the surf carrying the folbots on returning to the submarine.

"It is to be hoped that this operation, *the first of its kind involving the close co-operation of British naval, army and air units with our American Allies*, will be a happy augury for the future."

Jewell spent most of the 25th in *Maidstone* discussing details of his trip with Captain Fawkes and taking his first bath for several days. In the evening he was ordered to stand by for another secret mission. Somehow, he knew it was concerned with General Clark's promise: "I shall have another job for you soon."

CHAPTER FOUR

OPERATION KINGPIN

K EY principle in the concept of "Torch" had been the hope that a Frenchman could be found of such political integrity, patriotism and military renown that the varying factions in North Africa would rally to him and on the side of the Allies.

At the "white house with the red-tiled roof" on the coast, General Mast had been able to guarantee the loyalty of only the Algerian garrison he commanded. In his opinion, the forces at Oran and Casablanca were strongly pro-Vichy and would follow the orders of Pétain. Only one man could change their loyalty in a call to arms for a revival of France's military glory and weld all Frenchmen in North Africa under his standard to the Allied cause—General Henri Honoré Giraud, the very tall, spare and gaunt-faced hero of Wassigny on the Belgian frontier.

Giraud, a prisoner of war in Germany for two years, had escaped some six months before and was now sitting uneasily in Vichy France while Pétain and Laval planned to hand him back to the Germans in exchange for further concessions from Hitler. The Allied need for him in France had already been communicated to Mast by Robert Murphy and this had been relayed by secret courier to Lyons, where Giraud was living with his wife and family. The General had replied that he was willing to be smuggled from France to North Africa only if the Allies pledged to him a command in keeping with his rank and reputation. This was but a foretaste of the fierce patriotism, pride and dignity with which Giraud was to colour all his dealings with Mark Clark and Eisenhower in the weeks ahead.

Clark had explained to Mast that he was authorised to offer Giraud the command of all French Forces in Africa if he set up headquarters in Algiers prior to the landings and arranged for all key garrisons from Casablanca to Bone to be freely occupied by the invasion forces. Mast had promised to pass this on to Giraud, and Murphy would transmit the reply to Eisenhower.

Clark had added that an aircraft, surface ship or submarine would be placed at the General's disposal to help his escape from France.

Now, on October 25th while the "Torch" planners gave the green light for the invasion forces to gather at Gibraltar, General Eisenhower sent the following cable to President Roosevelt and the Secretary of State in Washington:

"In conference with AGREE (Clark) it develops that we will know within three days if KINGPIN (Giraud) is willing to move. If his decision is favourable his evacuation must take place not later than November 1st. French insist that he be taken from France in an American submarine but unless such a vessel is immediately available the time factor will force us to the undesirable alternative of using a British submarine which, in this event, must be placed under the nominal command of an American naval officer and will fly the American flag night and day throughout the operation to pacify KINGPIN.

"Arrangements have already been made to earmark a British submarine at Gibraltar for this purpose and a few additional United States officers and naval ratings will be flown by air to Gibraltar for the operation."

This stressing of his emphatic refusal to deal with the British gave some indication that Giraud was to be handled carefully indeed if all the plans for saving French, British and American lives were to be kept intact. There was no American submarine within 3,000 miles of Gibraltar, and *Seraph* was the obvious choice to be placed under American command. The important principle was that she should not only "be American" but "appear American" in Giraud's eyes. It was highly likely that, at the slightest sign of anything British, he would refuse to board and return to Lyons.

The following day Eisenhower approved a letter to Murphy containing the conditions under which Giraud would be rescued:

"You can inform KINGPIN that during those phases of the operation (Torch) that involve landing, establishing the security of French North Africa and providing necessary bases, it is considered essential that the American command organisation which has been set up with so much effort and difficulty for this special operation should remain unchanged.

"By the time this is accomplished it is to be assumed that the French forces, reinforced with material support from the Allied nations, will be sufficiently strong to ensure the complete security of French territory. French North Africa will then be turned over to French command.

"You should also expedite news of KINGPIN's decision. If favourable furnish complete details for his evacuation which must take place very soon. Since it is impossible for an American submarine to arrive in time, I have arranged for a British submarine under American command to stand by at Gibraltar to proceed at short notice upon receipt of orders from me. You should not mention this to Mast or KINGPIN."

Later that day, a signal was sent to Gibraltar formally requesting that *Seraph* be placed under the command of an American naval officer then visiting the Rock and held ready for immediate operations. This was the job Clark had promised Jewell when he had transferred to the Catalina.

At this stage Captain Fawkes reported to Admiral Collins and the Governor that their influence should be used to persuade Eisenhower to nominate another American officer for the command of *Seraph*. The officer named in Eisenhower's signal had earned for himself an unenviable reputation among his own compatriots as well as the Royal Navy in Gibraltar, and Fawkes was ready to fight his appointment to *Seraph* to the extent of making himself unpopular with the Americans and his own superiors.

He outlined his reasons to Admiral Collins who supported him in an official objection to the Admiralty. "Why," asked Fawkes, "can't you send Jerry Wright? He knows the ship and is liked by the men and if we let Jewell remain in working command it won't matter that he is a bit rusty on submarine procedure. Incidentally, if you are sending a French interpreter too, why not let Julius Holmes come out with Wright?"

In London, Eisenhower and Clark were more than ready to compromise rather than let personalities endanger an already delicate operation. The American naval officer's appointment was cancelled, and Jerry Wright was told to fly out to Gibraltar next morning. It was found that Julius Holmes was too involved in "Torch" planning to be spared from London and at his suggestion a signal was sent from London to Admiral Collins:

"Request Lieutenant-Colonel Bradley Gaylord 12th Air Force, now at Gibraltar, may be informed that General Eisenhower wishes him to accompany Captain Wright U.S.N., on Operation KINGPIN."

At 3 p.m. on the 27th Colonel Gaylord was sitting in his operations shack at the Rock airfield when the telephone rang and Major Tony Quayle, aide-de-camp to the Governor, asked: "If you hurry, how long will it take you to get up to Government House?"

"About seven minutes."

"Well, don't make it more than ten. There's someone here who wants to see you. It's important."

"Okay, I'll be right up."

Seven minutes later, Gaylord met Quayle at the entrance to Government House and was led direct to the Aide's bedroom. There, to his amazement, he found Jerry Wright well hidden from the eyes of Axis agents and with a broad grin spread across his face.

"Did you get Ike's message?" asked Wright.

"Yeah, but what are the details? How do we go about it?"

"It's simple. All we have to do is to go by submarine to the south of France and pick up a very important guy called Giraud and take him to Africa. Holmes says your French is pretty good. Can do?"

Aghast at the thought of an air force officer travelling at the ceilings normally attained by submarines, Gaylord nodded.

"Can you speak the lingo well enough to get us out of trouble on the beaches?" Gaylord assured him that his French was most suited to the waterfronts. Then Wright told him to pack his gear and board *Maidstone* where Captain Fawkes would give them dinner before going aboard the submarine.

That evening Bradley Gaylord, known to his friends as Brad, joined the "North African Canoeists Club"—that exclusive circle of American officers who wanted *Seraph* to help them carry out the "crazy stunts" which an official history has since called "the two special operations which did more to rejuvenate the fighting spirit of France and bring about the downfall of Mussolini than the actual landings themselves."

In his diary, Gaylord wrote:

"At dinner aboard *Maidstone* that night I met for the first time—and I am glad to say not the last—Captain Barney Fawkes, Britain's submarine chief at Gibraltar. He was a perfect host and revealed himself later as an efficient mastermind of tricky operations. He was delighted at meeting Jerry again and suggested we had one of his special cocktails."

Gaylord was no mean mixer of cocktails himself and it was as such that he was introduced to Bill Jewell who had just walked in at Fawkes's invitation to meet his passengers. After the introductions, Wright said:

"We're damn lucky to have Brad along, Bill."

Jewell was immediately interested. He had come to expect the Americans to have an expert in almost every field of war.

"That sounds good, providing he doesn't bring too much special equipment with him. We are pretty tightly packed now."

Wright gave a loud chuckle. "All the equipment he needs you've got in that Wardroom cupboard, Bill." Then, in a voice akin to reverence; "He puts together the best damn drink you ever tasted, boy."

Jewell should have known his Americans well enough to expect something like that.

After dinner, Fawkes, who had been kept fully informed of developments from London, gave them a briefing. Giraud's final decision had not yet reached London but it had been decided that with only eight days to go before the Expeditionary Force sailed from Gibraltar, the submarine should proceed to the south of France area and wait for further instructions.

They were to sail that evening with Jerry Wright in nominal command by order of Eisenhower and with the approval of the Admiralty and the Navy Department in Washington. *Seraph* would proceed to the Gulf of Lyons from which any point on the southern coast of France could be reached easily and was to return with Giraud along a clearly defined line to Gibraltar. On successive days a Catalina aircraft would fly along that line at a certain time to act as escort, or if it proved necessary to facilitate the arrival of Giraud in North Africa.

When the details had been explained, Fawkes called for a last drink and turned to Wright.

"By the way, Jerry, I nearly forgot a rather important

ceremony which is always performed when a Royal Navy officer is given a command. It won't last long, so please play ball for a minute. Will you stand with me, please."

The two officers stood facing each other and Fawkes produced from his pocket a scroll of paper tied with red tape and sealed with an impressive-looking stamp.

"Captain Jerauld Wright of the United States Navy, I am commanded by Their Lordships of the Board of Admiralty to inform you that you are hereby commissioned to take command of His Majesty's submarine, *Seraph*. You will at all times command her in the best interests of your sovereign and conduct her operations to the benefit of the British Commonwealth and Empire." He relaxed his suitably solemn expression and with a broad grin handed over the scroll.

Wright smiled back at him, glanced sympathetically at Jewell but his face suddenly went dark with suspicion.

"Hey Barney, hand over that commission, let's have a look at it." Hurriedly he broke the seal, untied the tape and opened it on the table. There for all to see was one of the most uncovered girls Varga had ever drawn for a well-known American magazine.

He joined the others in the general laughter. At the same time he carefully folded the Varga girl and put her in his pocket.

Earlier that afternoon, Captain Fawkes had inspected *Seraph* to check that she was ready for sea. The crew had been mustered for an address in which he had said:

"Now you are going on another special operation. It is to rescue a very important person from the French coast. The Germans want him badly so there might be trouble.

"Most important is that this submarine should be in all respects American. You have had Captain Wright aboard before. Now he is coming with you again, this time in actual nominal command, but Lieutenant Jewell is still your commanding officer and he will work the ship. For a short period while you are picking up your passengers, Captain Wright will be in complete command. At that moment I want you all who might be in sight of this passenger to behave as if you were American." He began returning the grins appearing before him. "And if you can speak their language, practise it and get a good twang or drawl into your voices.

"Now I wish you all in the U.S.S. *Seraph* a successful voyage."

The crew enjoyed that. Seraphese had been unofficial for several days. Now it had official blessing, though none dared tempt the fates by carrying it too far with Bill Jewell.

Jewell left *Maidstone* a few minutes before Wright and Gaylord to have the crew piped to sea stations and to make sure that the Commando trio, who had been ordered to stay aboard *Seraph* for the last two days in readiness for the operation, were fully prepared.

Jumbo Courtney was smoking on the conning tower as he crossed the gangplank. "Hi, Bill. What's happening?" Jewell explained.

"What, another goddam General!" shouted Courtney.

Then Jewell suddenly remembered something else.

"Jerry Wright's coming with us and we're flying the Stars and Stripes when we're up, of course, come night or day. He brought Colonel Gaylord of the United States Army Air Force."

"What's Gaylord coming for?"

"Well," grinned Jewell, "he makes the best damn' drink you ever tasted, boy."

Courtney registered no surprise. Instead, in a brightened tone, he commented:

"That's fine, the other reasons don't really matter."

Just then the two American officers arrived aboard and, in accordance with previous instructions, Spender, the First Lieutenant, ordered the Stars and Stripes to be hoisted. If Giraud's personal agents or Axis spies were watching they would note than an American submarine had left harbour that night.

As *Seraph* was casting off, a gramophone began blaring from the bowels of the *Maidstone* a tune recognised by one wit as "Yours". It was the wartime "Sweetheart of the Forces" Vera Lynn, singing the favourite nostalgic song of the day.

"Say, you *Maidstone* guys," twanged the rating, "send that dame over here. We need some female company to entertain the crew." When the singer reached the line: "Yours, till the end of life's story," he reverted to pure English. "That's a bloody fine send-off that is, I don't think."

Wright and Gaylord left the bridge and went aft to the

Wardroom where the newcomer was shown around by the "old hand at this submarine lark".

As soon as *Seraph* had cleared the harbour a cable was sent from *Maidstone* to Eisenhower:

"*Seraph sailed at 2100/27 with Captain Jerauld Wright, United States Navy, in command. Destination is Gulf of Lyons for further orders.*"

While *Seraph* turned to head up the coast of Spain towards France, Captain Fawkes was preparing another of his flotilla to follow and take over the operation should the enemy interfere and cause Wright to miss the rendezvous. Giraud was too important to the Allies at that particular moment for all the eggs to be carried in *Seraph*. The second basket, H.M.S. *Sybil*, commanded by Lieutenant E. J. D. Turner, sailed next morning to take her place if *Seraph* should scramble hers.

CHAPTER FIVE

KINGPIN'S ESCAPE

GENERAL HENRI HONORÉ GIRAUD, was no stranger to Germany or the Germans. In 1916, as a dashing cavalry officer, his enormous, distinguished moustache had spread across many of the Kaiser's newspapers which played him up as an important captive without whom a crack French regiment would lose its bite. A year later, he made headlines again when he escaped from his prison camp, picked up a stray horse and galloped out of Germany to rejoin the regiment. During this escape a bullet gave him a limp for life.

In May, 1940, he became the potential saviour of France when he took command of the broken French armies on the Belgian-Dutch frontier with his headquarters at Wassigny. For a few hours his arrival raised Allied hopes that the tide of steel from Germany would be halted suddenly. Instead the Nazis swept on, the French reeled back and Giraud's headquarters became an Allied outpost in conquered territory.

He held out with his headquarters staff of clerks, quartermasters and cooks for three days while the Panzer ocean lapped around him. Then it was every man for himself and, with one aide, Lieutenant Tannery, Giraud set out to march back to French lines. This proved an almost impossible task as the Allies were falling back faster than he could march and after two more days, he gave up, his game leg unable to carry the gaunt frame any further.

An hour or so later, German tanks trundled down the road and Giraud became a prisoner for the second time in his career. He was taken in a staff car to divisional headquarters and there he formally surrendered to the division commander, General Rommel.

A few days later Giraud was housed in Koenigstein Castle, a medieval fortress in the Elbe valley said to be escape-proof; and once more his flowing moustache occupied much space in German newspapers. His prison was a grim-looking castle with its grey-stone walls perched high on the brink of a

100-foot precipice. In such a place the Germans were convinced there was no possibility of the General repeating his escape of the earlier war.

He was in excellent company—120 French generals were imprisoned at Koenigstein and as Giraud was the most senior he commanded not only respect from the German commandant, but a really impressive guard of honour for ceremonial occasions.

There is inevitably one flaw in deeming escape impossible from castle or camp: the "impregnability complex" causes discipline among the guards to become more relaxed and the checking process is not so strictly applied. Koenigstein was no exception; the commandant worked harder at ingratiating himself with the prisoners, particularly Giraud, than at guarding them. As a result, the restless General was allowed to roam freely in the castle grounds and to walk along the ramparts of the wall overlooking the cliff drop. There was neither hand nor toehold visible on the face of either wall or cliff and because of this it was unguarded. Here, Giraud decided, was the "blind" spot in the castle's escape defences. He embarked on a two-year scheme to return to France.

First he established contact with the French Resistance and his wife. After that he scrounged the string which wrapped every parcel entering the castle. From this he plaited a flimsy-looking rope which would hardly bear even his long, thin body on a fall of 150 feet from ramparts to ground. He developed a passion for strawberry jam and in the many jars sent to him were hidden coils of copper wire to reinforce his makeshift rope. When this was done he felt the odds to be swinging in his favour. He needed money, so he received quantities of gift parcels containing commodities in short supply; these were sold to the guards and the General's cash supply assumed proportions of wealth. From the guards he acquired an old pair of trousers and a trench-coat, while from another prisoner he borrowed a railway timetable covering all Germany.

By April, 1942, a month less than two years from his first meeting with Rommel he was ready to escape. Wearing his old trousers and trench-coat to hide his uniform jacket, with food and money hidden about his body and the homemade rope tucked down a sleeve, he walked one evening to the ramparts.

It was warm and sunny—ideal for a cross country walk. A young German officer approached him and began discussing the war. Giraud interrupted him. "Young man, you have often said you would like to take my photograph when the sun was right. Today the sun is right, so go and get your camera and I will pose."

The German scuttled off, and quickly Giraud slung his rope over the ramparts. To his relief it reached the ground. Now that the moment had come, it looked frail indeed while his body felt heavier than ever. He swung his legs over the wall and held on grimly. The next few seconds were interminable as he slid slowly downwards, the wire cutting into his hands until they bled. Then he was down and walking hurriedly across the fields to a small copse. Here he clipped his moustache until it was unrecognisable, brushed himself down and set off for the nearest railway station.

For the next two weeks, he zig-zagged his way across Germany, getting steadily further from his logical destination, France, and nearer to his actual objective—Switzerland. There was a series of close disasters, but always his fluent German, active brain and blatant impertinence saw him through to safety. And on April 28th, he crossed the Swiss border with a price of 100,000 gold marks on his head—he was always grateful for such recognition from the German police.

In Switzerland, the French Resistance supplied him with credentials which enabled him to cross peaceably into Vichy France where he made his way to his wife and family at their home in Lyons.

Once at home, Giraud was technically safe. Under international law there is no power by which an escaped prisoner of war who has resumed civilian life in his own country can be forced to return to his prisoner status. Giraud knew the Germans had suffered a severe blow to their pride by his escape, but he relied on his own rank and reputation to save him from re-arrest by the Gestapo or Vichy agents.

Once again his picture decorated the German press alongside stories which berated him for being foolhardy, denounced his escape as a betrayal of France and threatened that his continued liberty was an obstacle in the process of Franco-German co-operation.

E

Two weeks later, he answered his telephone to hear Marshal Pétain, President of Unoccupied France, say: "General Giraud, you are to report to Vichy tomorrow morning where you will see Herr Otto Abetz, the German Ambassador. He wants to see you and I order you to appear."

Giraud shrugged as he put down the receiver. He had to see the Germans some time; it might just as well be sooner than later. He travelled to Vichy.

The interview was short and hard. After the expected reproaches and recriminations, Abetz said flatly: "You are to return to Germany. It is quite impossible for you to remain at liberty any longer."

"On what grounds do you insist I go back to captivity?"

"On patriotic grounds. You should know that your recent little prank has annoyed my Government to the extent that your presence here has brought all diplomatic negotiation between France and Germany to a halt. If you value your country's future and your personal safety I suggest you obey me and make arrangements to leave France immediately."

The General bristled at the German's arrogance. With his back stiffly straight, he towered over Abetz, his recently re-grown moustache standing out like a sabre as he replied:

"You have no power to make me return to Germany. And please do not mention patriotism to me. I shall stay here and work for France in my own way—the France that I know, not the one you blackmail into obedience."

Abetz changed his tactics and resorted to bribery. "General Giraud, you are an officer of high integrity. My country considers you among our greatest enemies, therefore we insist on your return. If you go back to Koenigstein, my Government will release 50,000 French prisoners of war."

"If I accept that offer what guarantees have I got that you will keep your promise?"

"The word of Germany."

In that remark, Giraud saw how shallow were Abetz's motives. He replied: "I will go back, Herr Abetz, if Germany will release all the married French prisoners of war."

Abetz gasped. "But, General, do you know there are about 400,000 married prisoners."

"Of course I know. I shall stay at Lyons until they come

home and you have my word that I shall then return to Koenigstein."

Abetz shouted angrily: "General Giraud, I asked you to come here for a serious discussion of one of the most difficult situations between our countries since the Armistice. Now that you are treating the matter so lightly there is no point in continuing."

Giraud nodded, turned about and stalked from the room. He had nearly reached the end of the corridor, when the door of another office opened and Pierre Laval, Prime Minister in the Pétain Government, called out: "Please come in here for a minute, General Giraud.

He followed the Premier, wearing a stained white tie, and stood to attention. It was to be a formal discussion.

"Bonjour, mon General," said Laval.

"Bonjour, Laval," said Giraud, equally stiffly.

"General Giraud, I am greatly distressed to hear of the unfortunate outcome of your meeting with Herr Abetz. He has just spoken to me on the telephone about it. General, I must advise you that it is essential that you return to Germany."

It was patently obvious that Laval had arranged to be the second line of attack should Abetz fail.

"On what grounds, Laval."

The Premier shifted angrily in his chair. "Because you are injuring France by your presence and interfering with my policies designed to improve the conditions of our country."

Giraud gazed thoughtfully at Laval and said softly: "You are the person who is injuring France. As for your policies, I detest them." With that he opened the door and strode from the building.

For the next three months, Giraud rarely left the privacy of his home. He expected that at any time a knock on the door would herald the arrival of Vichy agents sent to hand him back to the Germans; or the Gestapo could easily send their own men to kidnap him. This danger was real indeed in those confused days.

In September the first rumours that the Allies were planning an invasion of North Africa reached the Giraud home. An old African campaigner himself, Giraud could discount many of the rumours and establish for himself the basic formula of the attack. At the beginning of October the first message arrived from Mast in Algiers asking for guidance on what stand he should take in the event of an invasion. Mast's problem was typical of many French consciences in that period of crisis— too often they ended in personal tragedy.

Through this first message, Giraud opened secret communication with Algiers; and among the first letters brought by courier was Mast's suggestion that if he would come to Algiers and rally all the garrisons to his colours, the Allies could enter North Africa freely and the Germans would be confronted with a *coup d'état*. It was a bold, dangerous plan from an officer who, though serving Pétain, still believed in an undefeated France.

Mast indicated that he was in touch with Allied headquarters through Robert Murphy and could negotiate in accordance with Giraud's wishes. Through this medium the deal was made to bring Giraud out of France to take over in North Africa as French Commander-in-Chief. Throughout the correspondence, however, Giraud, skilled and experienced soldier as he was, stressed his dislike of Britain, contempt for her Army and the firm belief that she alone had been responsible for his country's fate. He would have nothing to do with representatives of Britain, but would do business with the Americans. His second motive was even stranger and more remote from reality than his hatred of the British; he believed that the Americans, powerful in quantity of troops, equipment and production potential, lacked quality and would welcome him as Supreme Commander or at least could be persuaded to give him such an appointment.

In one letter, he said: "The Americans are amateurs at war, but they have the valuable asset of enthusiasm. They will recognise that France has always produced the finest soldiers of Europe and will be certain to accept my advice and leadership in the interests of total victory."

Giraud's decision to help the Allies was spurred by a threat from Vichy. The Resistance learned that a powerful effort was to be made to re-take the General as prisoner. It seemed likely that even the patriots who guarded his house so unobtrusively would be hard pressed to protect him. The sooner he left France the better, was the universal opinion of his friends.

Yet for weeks he bargained with the Allies through Mast and refused to believe that he would not be appointed Supreme Commander. Mast wrote: "I think you may be assured from my talks with Murphy that, once you arrive in Algiers, the Allies will see the military importance of your presence and accept that you are the only logical commander for the North African theatre."

Even at this stage, the French seemed unable to understand that Giraud's use to the Allies, while of tremendous importance, fell short of placing him in overall command.

It satisfied Giraud who made immediate plans to call together a small staff of officers whom he knew to be waiting for a chance to join the Allies. Yet he found time to stress in a further message to Mast that if a submarine of any nation other than America arrived he would refuse to embark. This was underlined in Mast's conversations with Robert Murphy.

Giraud's plans were not easily made. Vichy agents kept a strict watch on his house and he was required to report every four hours by day to the nearest police station to prove he was still in France. This routine was not only tiresome but also inconvenient to his escape. One day he pleaded illness and retired to bed, a Resistance doctor certifying that he was too ill to make his four-hourly walk to the police station. If they wanted to check on his presence they would have to visit the General at his house.

The police kept this up only briefly, getting bored as Giraud had known they would, at having to come up to his bedroom four times a day. His illness was prolonged until the police gave up and left him strictly alone.

When they did call again several days later on what they had now decided should be a weekly check, he was gone.

At that moment he was in Marseilles at Resistance Headquarters planning the last stage of his getaway. Messages flashed across southern France ordering police authorities to raid all homes occupied by people of dubious political sentiments. Giraud had just left the Marseilles headquarters with his staff when the police pounced, and the patriots had to fight a running battle before escaping through the backstreets. Because of this, the local Resistance leader was forced to catch up with Giraud's party and join them for the final escape.

Only an hour before the raid a message had been sent to London giving the time, place and date of the rendezvous. Now they sped in cars along the coast road towards Nice; but telephone calls had been made by the Marseilles police to all resorts on the coast with the warning that Giraud might be attempting to leave France that night.

At the tiny resort of Le Lavendou, the cars turned off the main road and parked near the railway station. There the party broke up, one group of five heading for Cap d'Antibes while Giraud and three more made for the beach. On the way through a small wood, they heard the sudden blast of police whistles and quickly fell under the protection of nearby bushes. It seemed they were about to be discovered within minutes of the final dash. The sound of heavily-booted feet and crackling bush came nearer as the net closed in.

At sea, *Seraph* was creeping towards the rendezvous.

CHAPTER SIX

SERAPH IS MISSING

FOR Colonel Gaylord, an Air Force officer to whom life was normal at 20,000 feet, it was distinctly abnormal at minus 40 feet.

"I felt most uncomfortable," he wrote in his diary, "and didn't dare think how old the crew of *Seraph* must have been. To Jerry Wright and I they were just a bunch of laughing young school kids. Of the officers, the only one not in his early twenties was 'Chiefie' Sutton, an old-timer in submarines with a twinkle in his eye who fixed all sorts of gadgets for everybody, took continuous verbal beatings about the terrible state of his motors and settled all arguments among the crew with remarkable results in raising morale.

"I had always heard of the good food in submarines and this was no exception. On the first day out, there were steaks for all hands at supper and we were warned to make the most of it as fresh food soon ran out and then we would have to revert to iron rations.

"After supper the first morning everybody tucked himself away and in due course I found myself in a comfortable bunk thinking submarine life not so bad and certainly not what I had always thought it to be like. My first impressions were that both officers and men were always busy and passengers were just so much extra baggage. The three Commandos and myself made the place a bit crowded, Jerry Wright having made one trip in her and now become her commander and in charge of the mission, no longer being counted as extra.

"The next day I realised how comfortable it was to travel at 40 feet below the surface. Aircraft were overhead hunting for submarines almost all day and it was nice to think of that great cushion of water between us and depth charges.

"After breakfast, in the evening, I climbed to the conning tower to have a look at the Mediterranean at night. I was told that if the klaxons went it meant we were diving and to get back inside unless I wanted to stay outside. Never mind barked shins or skinned knuckles—just get down that hole faster than you ever thought you could.

"What a sight it was on that conning tower. Here I was just a few feet above the water, plunging ahead with the beautiful Spanish coast stretching as far as the eye could see. How very different from everything I had expected. How could you have claustrophia among these smiling boys whose easy informality was so apparently a thin cover for the rigid discipline on which every man knows his life depends upon the other fellow. It is so completely infectious. You suddenly realise that here is one of the essential points about war: there is no substitute for good company. The boys in the Submarine Service convey a spirit which quickly explains why they would sooner be in submarines than anywhere else.

"Then we went below to look over the maps we had brought along. Bill, his navigator, Jerry and I started a guessing game as to where Giraud would want us to pick him up. Curiously we all agreed it could only be one of three places—somewhere just east of Marseilles, Cap d'Antibes or Nice."

Jewell thought this as good a time as any to explain to the Commandos that the deception scheme by which the ship became U.S.S. *Seraph* was no idle jest. He set the example by cheerfully acknowledging Wright as the senior officer of the mission and the nominal commander of *Seraph*.

"It seemed," said Jewell later, "more suitable for me to act the rôle of junior officer—the one who traditionally gets underfoot on the bridge. I implored Jerry, Gaylord and our soldier friends to regard me simply as a handyman called Bill upon whom they could all shove the care and responsibility of diving and surfacing the submarine."

The Commandos were obviously finding it difficult to grasp the idea that one of His Britannic Majesty's submarines could so easily become the property of another country. If the crew were also thinking deeply there was no sign of a verbal protest. They were sailors, these were orders, and with looks of resignation they accepted their temporary enrolment in the service of the United States. Wright and Gaylord, unable to resist the potentialities of the situation, moved adroitly into the attack.

With the innocuous comment that the mission would succeed only if Giraud were firmly convinced that an American submarine had been sent, they glanced around the Wardroom until their eyes rested on Courtney.

"I think it would be a good idea if Jumbo posed as the American captain and welcomed KINGPIN," said Gaylord to Wright with seeming innocence.

"You're perfectly right, Brad. But he'll have to keep up the pose and handle *Seraph* as if he really is her skipper," replied Jerry.

Courtney chipped in brightly: "That's going to be easy if Bill will stay at my elbow in case I have to do something with her."

"As good an idea as you've ever had," Jewell intervened. "I'll be so close to your elbow I'll thank you to pad the ugly thing."

"Quite right," approved Brad Gaylord benignly. "And I think, Captain Courtney, it might add to the effect if you would take the trouble to learn a few American phrases. You could, for instance, greet him with 'Hi, general, what's cookin' on the front burner?' or something equally democratic."

Wright wrinkled his nose in distaste. "That's corny, Brad. 'What's buzzin', cousin?' would be more up to date."

A series of muffled chokes came from up for'ard and Jewell looked round the corner of the Wardroom to see a bunch of sailors who, having overheard parts of the conversation and unable to resist the rest, were listening intently. He turned back without saying anything.

"Jerry, you're too goddam meticulous," Gaylord was saying. "Giraud won't know how far we have progressed with the English language." Was it really likely, he demanded, that a Frenchman who spoke no English and recently domiciled in Germany would be *au courant* with the delicate nuances of American slang?

Then it was noticed that Jumbo was far away and his lips were moving silently as though he was seriously trying to memorise all the Americanisms he had ever heard. The incorrigible American pair hastily dropped all pretence and Wright confessed to their wickedness.

Jumbo counter-attacked indignantly. "And I suppose

General Eisenhower sent you along to mix cocktails," he said to Gaylord.

"I'm afraid not," replied the Air Force officer urbanely, "but I'll be only too delighted to whip something up when the time comes." And he looked longingly at the locked Wardroom cupboard.

From then on Jewell had to tolerate further practice in Americanisms from his crew who took to reporting on watch with a wide variety of accents which provided constant amusement to the only two real descendants of the New World colonists. Seraphese was rapidly becoming a novel and sometimes startling language; good enough, it was decided, to fool Giraud successfully.

"I hadn't thought of it before," recalls Gaylord, "but a submarine is a fine place for a rest cure. You can practically reach out of your bunk to have your meals off the table and there is plenty of time to sleep."

On the 30th, they were clear of friendly shores and any aircraft or surface vessel could safely be assumed to be enemy. *Seraph* submerged until dark when she surfaced again for fresh air and breakfast. Then Courtney repeated his parlour game of the previous mission by insisting that Wright and Gaylord practice boarding a folbot canoe off the Wardroom table.

This was mainly for the Air Force officer's benefit as Wright had shown on the previous trip how expert he was at handling these boats. Gaylord entered into the fun and soon managed to satisfy the perfectionist, Foote. Of them all that evening, only Livingstone, recently nicknamed 'Doc', seemed very unhappy about the whole affair.

He was a demolition and sabotage expert. All he wanted out of this war was to create big bangs. Unfortunately, big bangs were not planned for this operation. As on the previous voyage, Courtney and Livingstone rarely appeared together while on passage. Doc was miserable when *Seraph* plunged along on the surface giving slight kicks and rolling unsympathetically. Jumbo began to go green when travelling submerged by day. The unchanged air made him groggy.

Gaylord wrote of Livingstone: "He loved discussions on history, art and ethics, but he would end them all with a dreamy, lonesome look in his eyes as he murmured: 'Oh dear,

I wish we could do a job with a big, big bang.' Later he was to do a sabotage job in Italy and, when I asked one of his companions how it went off, he said I should have seen the light in Doc Livingstone's eyes when the train blew up in the middle of the bridge it was crossing. They had glowed with sheer contentment."

The next night Jumbo persuaded Wright and Jewell to let him carry out a proper run with the canoes. They were brought up through the fore hatch, laid alongside and Gaylord practised getting in and out with *Seraph* rolling unexpectedly and mischievously each time he had one foot in mid air. Then Foote and Courtney took one away into the night to test the walkie-talkie set and the infra-red signal lamps. These proved to be working, so they returned, stowed away the folbots and *Seraph* continued on her way thankful that the enemy could be expected to be sleeping at that time of night.

Before midnight, a signal was received from Captain Fawkes saying that Mark Clark had no news about the rendezvous yet. Only a few days were left to the invasion and it seemed reasonably certain that the great troop convoys were already forming up. The General had to be in North Africa before the landings.

Gaylord took comfort from Jewell, of whom he said later: "During this anxious period, the influence of Bill Jewell was clearly apparent. Quiet and reserved, he had little to say, but when some question came up he would nod his head, smile and then tell us exactly how he was going to do it—always with a glance at Jerry Wright, of course. His quiet air of confidence and authority had its influence over us all."

The same night they received a general signal announcing the date for the landings, November 8th, but they had been eight days at sea and had given up any hope of taking Giraud to North Africa. He would have to be taken to Gibraltar as fast as possible. It was November 4th and only four days to go. Wright and Jewell had decided that, once clear of the French coast after the mission had been accomplishd, they would signal Gibraltar to send an aircraft to take off the General. It would be up to someone else then to salvage something of his value even though he had not arrived in Africa.

Seraph surfaced as usual at dusk and, after giving his orders to the watch, Jewell joined the cribbage players in the Wardroom for breakfast. They ate in silence each occupied with his thoughts and worried about the lack of news. It had become almost a ritual for someone to ask: "Anything new?"

"No." And with a shake of heads, the business of eating would go on with the unanimous hope that the delicate negotiations between Eisenhower and Giraud had not foundered on the rocks of easily-offended French pride and the personal stubbornness of the fiery General.

Suddenly, at 8 p.m. the radio operator poked his head from his office next door to the Wardroom and with a smile announced the receipt of a message in code. There was a dive for code books, the table was cleared magically and the officers settled down to the maddeningly slow decoding procedure.

It was from Captain Fawkes and, if not decisive, at least it carried OPERATION KINGPIN somewhat nearer to reality.

"KINGPIN *with three others will be ready to embark in shoreboat from La Fosette, 1,000 yards east of Le Lavendou, tomorrow Thursday night. Shoreboat will flash 'S' for Sugar to seaward commencing* 2300 *Thursday, November 5th. You are to approach and leave rendezvous from east of La Lavendou.*

"*If weather permits Catalina aircraft will subsequently rendezvous with you to take off passengers. If operation not carried out Thursday-Friday night withdraw and prepare to carry out Friday-Saturday night. Informed by Their Lordships that many people in London interested in progress and wish to be kept fully informed of the state of your passengers. Further instructions may follow.*"

At last there was some action. A rapid check by the navigator showed they could be in position by 1100 the following morning—the day of the pick-up. *Seraph* picked up speed and stayed on the surface throughout the night, and at dawn the crew turned in for a brief rest until action stations were sounded a few minutes before the coastline came in view through the periscope. She approached to within 500 yards and Jewell handed over the periscope to the Commandos who took turns at making themselves familiar with the shore and its various distinguishing points in case they would have to land that night.

Afterwards they withdrew to the Wardroom to contemplate

whatever mayhem and massacre they might be able to cause should their presence ashore be required. There was no doubt in any mind that the soldiers sincerely hoped Laval and Himmler would turn up instead of Giraud. At the same time the thorough Jumbo quite seriously rehearsed his colleagues in Americanisms while a powerful doubt assailed Jewell.

"Suppose Giraud brings his own interpreter and Jumbo greets him with 'hi-ya, toots,' or something like that?" he inquired of Gaylord. "What will the interpreter do?"

"He'll throw in his hand and quit interpreting," predicted the Colonel confidently. "What else could the poor devil do?"

There was a constant coming and going of fishing boats around the hovering *Seraph*, but none came close enough to cause any real alarm. Every few minutes the periscope went up and there was no sign ashore of any undue inquisitiveness about what was happening to seaward.

At the same time, *Seraph*'s sister, *Sybil*, was approaching the same coast about 30 miles out, in accordance with a signal sent by Captain Fawkes to Lieutenant Turner. Giraud's rendezvous arrangements called for two pick-ups—he had divided his party to make certain some at least got through—and his officers were to embark the following night. He had not thought of the risk to the submarine in remaining so long in enemy waters. Fawkes's foresight in sending two submarines to the area was now apparent. *Sybil* was to make the second rendezvous. In a signal to Turner, he said:

"You are to rendezvous with shoreboat carrying ten passengers which will be 800 yards off La Fosette at midnight on November 8th. Boat will flash 'K' for King and you should reply with 'K' for King on a dimmed blue light. P-219 is carrying out similar mission on night November 5-6th."

Sybil followed her sister shorewards at a speed calculated to let *Seraph* get clear before she approached the coast.

After dark on the 5th, *Seraph* surfaced to find a rough sea running. Lights came from the shore only a few hundred yards away. Occasionally car headlights lit up the sea brilliantly as the road twisted and turned out of Le Lavendou. The seraphim were gloomy indeed at the chances of the mission being carried out in such foul weather. It seemed unlikely that even such a determined adventurer as Giraud would risk his lame leg in transferring from a small boat to the slippery deck of a pitching and tossing submarine.

Rendezvous time came and passed; it seemed their fears were well grounded. At that moment a stream of lights approached from the shore—a fleet of trawlers heading for the fishing grounds and steering a course straight for *Seraph*. Klaxons sounded and the conning tower crew with Wright sandwiched in the middle galloped down to the control room as she submerged in thirty seconds. Fifteen minutes later *Seraph* had scraped herself along the bottom underneath the fishermen and surfaced again, this time only 400 yards from the beach.

It was now half an hour after the rendezvous time and they worried again that Giraud's boat might have been turned back by the fishing fleet. Then another signal came from Barney Fawkes at Gibraltar:

"Rendezvous with KINGPIN *may be as late as one hour. His boat to come 800 yards to seaward before making recognition signal. (You are to identify yourself by flashing 'S' for Sugar on a dimmed blue light.")*

Something had happened ashore, but what puzzled the crew was how the delay message had reached the Allies. Fawkes was being kept informed by London who presumably were being briefed by Giraud. In fact, Giraud was in radio contact with Murphy and Mast in Algiers who were in touch with London. Meanwhile, General Clark had arrived with Eisenhower at Gibraltar and messages were going direct to him from Algiers. A few minutes later another signal was received from Gibraltar saying:

*"*KINGPIN *confirms he will be at rendezvous tonight but may be about one hour late. In the event of danger from enemy, signalling will be interrupted. Codeword for pick-up is* MINERVA *but it is not clear this end if he intends that as a password."*

It was abundantly clear that few Englishmen could say "Minerva" with an accurate American accent, so Wright elected to leave Jewell on the bridge while he went down to the fore casing to greet the General. In any event, he had to make a great display of the United States Navy stripes on his sleeves.

Meanwhile, weather reports were received which stressed that conditions off the south of France would deteriorate fast.

About two hours of present roughness could be expected, after which it would become worse. *Seraph* hung on to her position in the hope that the rendezvous would be made by KINGPIN inside the next two hours.

As the minutes went by, the sea grew steadily rougher and, at Jewell's suggestion, Bolton, who was to be in charge of the embarking operations on the fore deck, went below and changed into bathing trunks and plimsoll slippers. Gaylord, who was to assist him and make the most of using his voice, changed into a similar rig. When they returned to the bridge, the suspense increased, as Wright drew their attention to odd flickering lights in a large house ashore overlooking the front.

In the woods, Giraud and his staff hugged the ground under the bushes as the searchers approached. Their bush was hit by sticks, dry leaves and twigs snapped under heavy boots, and then the police had passed. Exultant, the party crept forward to the back of a house. A series of knocks and a door was opened to let them in. Cups of soup passed round and their host flashed a torch seawards through a window. An anxious discussion followed, and last messages were left behind for delivery to friends and relatives. Soon a burly, heavily-muffled fisherman beckoned them to follow him outside. He led them across the front, down to the beach and out along a small pier to which a tiny rowing boat was tied. The four of them jumped in, the fishermen threw off the ropes and grabbed the oars, and steadily pulled seawards.

On *Seraph*'s bridge a signalman read the flashes from the house ashore—O-N-E—H-O-U-R. It was then midnight and Bolton and Gaylord were beginning to shiver in their bathing trunks. An air of despondency settled over *Seraph*. Suddenly a look-out sighted a darkened ship out to sea about three miles away. Binoculars swung round and hearts stopped beating as an E-boat was seen cutting through the sea on her patrol. Jewell's immediate reaction was to dive; but he remembered in time that to dive now would probably mean failure to contact Giraud and a miserable end to the whole operation.

Wright read his thoughts, tapped him on the shoulder and shook his head. Jewell nodded and they watched the enemy draw closer. *Seraph* presented a small silhouette but it seemed impossible for her to escape detection. Fervent silent prayers were offered that Giraud would not start signalling and attract the enemy's attention. The minutes dragged and the enemy seemed to be slowing down. All movement in the submarine stopped and the engines were silenced. Five minutes of eternity ticked before the E-boat vanished into the shadows, the faint sound of her powerful motors subsiding until there was only the slap of the angry sea at *Seraph*'s sides. Her engines were started again and she pointed at the beach, the conning-tower crew relaxing with deep sighs of relief. It had been too close and there was no stomach for further jest or banter.

Grimly they waited for Giraud—or the enemy. The signal from the house had not been part of the programme, either, and the Commandos stood around the conning tower armed with tommy-guns and grenades ready to blast into action should the enemy try and spring his trap. Time seemed to stand still until at last the look-outs, upon whom a submarine relies for safety, reported something moving at a jetty ashore. It was nearly one o'clock when they both reported again that a boat was pulling from the jetty. A cross wind was blowing up and, now that zero hour was approaching, not much time would be left before the weather made embarkation impossible.

All the bridge personnel could now see the boat. It was painted white and about 100 yards from the shore began signalling with a dim light. This was the correct recognition signal, but *Seraph* was reluctant to reply, hoping she would be seen without having to disclose her position not only to the Giraud party but also to any watchers ashore. Then it became obvious that the boat was heading in the wrong direction and would miss her unless something was done to attract attention. There was no room in the shallow, rock-strewn water to manœuvre across and intercept. With some misgivings, Wright ordered the reply to be given on a dimmed lamp.

It was seen immediately and the small, white boat swung round. Spray was flying round the fore deck from the choppy sea as Wright, Gaylord and Bolton left the conning tower to join the embarkation party on the deck casing. Only a few inches below the surface were the big bulges of the ballast tanks. The five members of the crew tied lifelines round the

Americans in case of accidents. Then the white rowing boat came out of the shadows and was clearly revealed in the moonlight.

Colonel Gaylord's first impressions were recorded in his diary. "It was one of those old French fishing boats about as broad in the beam as it was long. It was painted white, with red paint round the gunwales and on the seat. Sitting in the bow was an old fisherman. How he ever kept that boat under way alone in that sea I shall never know. In the stern sat General Giraud— 6 feet odd, dressed in civilian clothes and wearing a grey fedora. His gloved hands were folded over a walking stick and a rain-coat was thrown over his shoulders like a cloak. It was the first time I had ever seen him and he looked rather like an old-time monarch visiting his fleet.

"He appeared then, as he did at all times, to be a man with great dignity. The other three in the boat looked all huddled together and none too happy—which was only too true."

The *Seraph*'s crew threw a line across to the boat and began to pull it alongside, but the sea was too strong and Wright and Gaylord had to add their weight before the boat swung round abreast of the submarine and drifted closer. Gaylord saw that it was about to bump hard against the casing and yelled for everyone to stop heaving. If anyone were caught between the two vessels as they hit, a nasty mess could be the only result.

As the boat hit the submarine, Giraud stood up, put one foot on the gunwale of the fishing boat and made a great leap as the two vessels rebounded apart after the bump. He missed *Seraph*'s deck and went down between the fishing boat and the submarine. Luckily, he landed on the ballast tanks just below the surface and those within reaching distance grabbed him. He was dragged safely on to the casing just before the fishing boat came crashing alongside for the second time. When Giraud stood up, he seemed quite unconcerned and shook hands formally with Captain Wright who, with Gaylord interpreting, welcomed him aboard the U.S.S. *Seraph*. The ropes were let go, the fisherman waved and pulled his brave little boat into the heavy sea to disappear into the night.

Jewell gave his orders softly from the bridge and *Seraph* turned about to move into the heavy sea to the safety of wide

F

open spaces. She had been confined for too long in dangerous shallow waters under the eyes and ears of the enemy.

Seraph's swing seawards had the effect of sinking her stern slightly and a shallow flood of black water boiled for'ard in the direction of the guests escorted by Wright and Gaylord. From the bridge it looked as if they were about to be washed overboard, but they saw the danger and scampered up the conning tower footholds.

Jewell saluted Giraud, but force of habit made him forget his rôle as a junior officer in an American submarine and he offered the greeting usually given by a captain. "Welcome aboard, sir," he said in his best English and was rewarded by a dirty look from Wright and a chuckle from Gaylord. The General nodded, smiled and said: "*Merci, M'sieur*," as though he understood perfectly. Jewell's momentary astonishment gave way to the comforting thought that greetings in any language were mostly understandable. For a minute, he wondered what Giraud would do if he unmasked the deception —he could but jump overboard and swim back to France if his anti-British complex was powerful enough, and a man who had escaped from the Koenigstein to the south of France might do just that. Jewell decided to say as little as possible until *Seraph* was well outside swimming distance. A few minutes later, she dived and Jewell made his way to join the party in the Wardroom reflecting sourly that his submarine was becoming more like Victoria Station every trip.

Gaylord whispered a request that, as everyone was soaking wet, he should unlock the drink cupboard. Jewell nodded agreement. The Colonel promptly got busy with cocktail shaker and glasses, proving his professional skill beyond doubt. In the belief that this was to be his one opportunity to use the ingredients produced from the cupboard he mixed bottles freely.

With Giraud were his son Léon, his Chief of Staff, Captain André Beaufré, and an aide, Lieutenant Viret of the French Navy. Drinks were passed round, toasts offered loudly by the American officers and mumbled by the British while the Frenchmen replied in their own language.

With Gaylord acting as interpreter and Beaufré, who appeared to speak a little English assisting, the General began plying Wright with questions, his choice making it certain that he had accepted the submarine as American. He apologised for keeping them waiting, told the story of the attempted ambush ashore and asked about the invasion. When told it was only three days off, he was shocked and murmured that he had hoped to persuade the Allies to concentrate on landing in Southern France.

At this point, Courtney decided it was high time to try out his seraphese and, looking Captain Beaufré straight in the eye, he drawled: "Say, Captain, you people must be goddam tired. I reckon you should save the gabbin' till tomorrow, hit the hay right now and grab yourselves a right useful slice of shut-eye."

The French officer's eyebrows shot up in amazement and Gaylord had to intervene hastily to put the idea of sleep across more simply to Giraud who quickly agreed. Jumbo looked at the Colonel sulkily, muttered something about "having heard him say exactly that himself" and wandered off to stow away his guns.

Now that Giraud was safely aboard, Wright revealed that the submarine was H.M.S. *Seraph* and identified himself finally as a member of Eisenhower's staff. Giraud seemed unaffected by the disclosure.

Later, Jewell saw the French guests tucked away in their bunks and the other officers in the secondary wardroom before going forward to talk softly with the officer on watch in the glow of the red lamps which were the only lighting at night. The U.S.S. *Seraph* was well clear of the coast and he could turn in himself before the time came to signal Gibraltar that the operation had been successfully completed with KINGPIN safely aboard.

Seraph's sailing orders said she was to signal Gibraltar after crossing a line some seventy miles away from the coast. As soon as she had given her position, course and speed an aircraft would be sent to rendezvous with her to take off the passengers. In any event, she was to head for Gibraltar along an agreed line above which the aircraft would fly at night. Above all, *Seraph* was to stay submerged by day as at this critical moment in the planning of "Torch" all Allied aircraft had been ordered to bomb submarines on sight.

When the Frenchmen had retired, silence fell in the Wardroom until some time later three of *Seraph*'s officers—Spender,

Edsell and Bolton—sat round the table and began to talk in quiet, conversational tones. After gossiping about the day's events, they came inevitably to the plan to dupe the guests into believing they were aboard an American submarine. Unaware of Wright's disclosure to Giraud, they joked delightedly about the hoax, and how it had fooled the General, and concocted hare-brained schemes to ensure that the ruse was successfully continued.

They were momentarily startled by the sound of movement from Jewell's bunk but soon finished talking in the safe knowledge that Giraud could not speak English. Afraid, however, that they were disturbing him they departed to the control room where they told Jewell of the incident and their possible indiscretion.

The Frenchmen rose early, attacked a hearty meal and, after being told that smoking was forbidden in a submerged submarine, settled down for a chat. Suddenly, a group of red-faced officers gazed with pop-eyed consternation at Giraud who, with no explanation of how he had mastered the language overnight, began to speak not only in English, but in the fluent variety normally used on the playing fields of Eton. But fears of any angry outburst faded as he gave not a sign in speech or manner that he had overheard the truth of the deception the night before. And none of his listeners quite dared to ask him if he had. If he was decent enough to ignore it, then it was best forgotten. Shameful glances were cast towards the deck when it was found that all the Frenchmen spoke good English. Now that the language difficulty had been broken down and there was no further need of pretence, Gaylord's offer to mix another round of his specials was accepted.

Wright told the story of a young British submarine commander who had fired a torpedo by mistake at a whale. He chuckled at his own story despite protests from Jewell who, to ward off the next part of the joke, said hurriedly: "I ought to know. After all I did it myself, once."

"No," said Gaylord, incredulously. "Did you hit it, Bill?"

"What a question," put in Wright. "Of course he hit it. Even you couldn't miss a whale, Brad. Not with a shot-gun, anyway."

This elevating discussion was interrupted by the wireless

operator who handed Wright a signal. It was from Fawkes and gave the contents of a broadcast Eisenhower would require Giraud to make to North Africa from Gibraltar calling on all French forces to fight alongside the Allies when they landed. Giraud was asked to approve the text which would be released as soon as he arrived.

The Wardroom was still as Wright read out the proposed text and ended by laying the signal before Giraud. They looked at the General with painful intensity as his grave face glanced back at each in turn. Then he spoke with quiet firmness and impressive dignity.

"I am a soldier, not a politician," he said slowly. "I cannot authorise the release of such a statement or make a broadcast on these lines." His voice dropped to a near whisper and, as if to himself, he muttered: "I must think of France—only of France."

For the rest of the day, Wright and Gaylord were left alone with the Frenchmen to try to persuade the General to change his mind. He was adamant in his determination to avoid the political issues involved in Eisenhower's draft. Even Captain Beaufré, who took the Allied side, could not move him.

Giraud never did vary from that fundamental philosophy. He believed that most of Europe's troubles were caused by military men invading the field of politics and the most they could extract from him after hours of argument was a promise that he would issue orders to North Africa from which anyone could draw whatever political conclusions they liked.

With this Wright and Gaylord had to be content and, as *Seraph* was nearing the point at which she could break radio silence, a condensation of the discussions was included in the signal Jewell proposed sending to Captain Fawkes.

Seraph surfaced at dusk, the usual rush of fresh air cleaned out smells and the cook began to prepare breakfast. At 10 p.m. Jewell ordered the wireless operator to start sending his report to Gibraltar. This would be the first news of Giraud's escape and would at the same time start a mild panic at Headquarters with his refusal to authorise the political broadcast.

A few minutes later the wireless operator returned to the bridge: "I'm sorry, sir, but the transmitter has broken down."

This was the worst possible misfortune but Jewell nodded

and told the rating to do his best. The word soon spread around the ship and a strange uneasiness communicated itself without words. From the Wardroom Gaylord noticed the wireless operator leave his room with an arm badly skinned below the elbow. He mentioned it to the rest of the passengers but it was dismissed as an injury received through some careless accident. At midnight when the fault was still undiscovered, Jewell came down to break the news himself.

"Good Lord," exclaimed Gaylord, "Can't we fix the transmitter, somehow?"

"We're trying now, but it might take quite a while."

By dawn the cantankerous transmitter still refused to work and the position began to look black. The landings were due to take place the next night. If Giraud had to stay aboard *Seraph*, he would not get to Gibraltar before the 11th—too late to be of much use to the Allies. Even worse was the thought that, as from the next day, the western Mediterranean would be filled with warships, convoys, anti-submarine patrols and aircraft. All would be searching for submarines who could not give the correct identification signals by radio and would therefore be legitimate targets.

Meanwhile, Captain Fawkes voiced his fears on the telephone to Mark Clark, now occupying an office inside the Rock, that *Seraph* might be missing. She was ten hours overdue in making her radio report. Her wireless equipment had been carefully checked before she sailed and only damage caused by enemy action could have put it out of use.

It was the first time that Captain Fawkes had ever experienced the possibility of having to report one of his own submarines as missing and it affected him more deeply than he had thought possible. An experienced submariner himself, he knew the risks faced by his submarines and had schooled himself to regard them cynically as being either successful or unlucky. Bill Jewell had become a favourite commander; the other officers and crew he knew well. Wright and Gaylord he could count now among his personal friends. Then there was the importance of Giraud to the Allies. With Giraud gone, would General Mast carry on with his promise to allow the invasion forces free entry into Algiers—or would there be bloody fighting with thousands dead? All this had hinged on the submarine.

Now that he had to regard them as officially missing he still shared with Mark Clark the faint hope that there was some simple explanation for *Seraph*'s silence. The Catalina aircraft scheduled to fly along her line of passage home was flown off. There was nothing to do but wait.

Jewell, Wright and Gaylord stood on the conning tower bridge watching dawn rise on Friday the 7th. Everyone aboard who had even the remotest idea of how radios worked had been called in to help trace the fault in the transmitter. *Seraph* was proceeding along the route home laid down in her sailing orders and approaching that part of the Mediterranean where both enemy and friendly air and sea patrols would be attacking submarines on sight. The three officers looked at the east where already the rising of the sun was driving the darkness before it. In a few minutes it would be time to dive unless they invited trouble by staying on the surface—and with Giraud aboard that might spell disaster.

Suddenly Jewell said: "We are in trouble; and when we are in trouble someone has to make a mistake. I think it had better be me. We will stay on the surface today and see if that blasted aircraft can't spot us."

His companions were silent for a moment, turning over the significance of this matter-of-fact pronouncement. Then Gaylord blurted out: "Good for you, Bill."

Wright grinned and said: "You're right. Now all we need is some luck."

Jewell ordered the officer of watch to double the look-outs and emphasised the importance of a strict air watch. When the extra watch arrived it became uncomfortably crowded on the bridge—if thoughts strayed to the muddle that would follow the need to dive. Then Wright suggested they go below for a cup of coffee and Jewell remarked to the O.O.W.: "From now on its catch as catch can. Just make sure we catch the right bird."

In his Patrol Report, Jewell wrote: "I decided to remain on the surface despite all orders to the contrary, because it seemed important to me to get KINGPIN or a message through to Gibraltar as quickly as possible. If we failed to sight the Catalina, we might get through to a passing Allied plane which could then inform Gibraltar of our predicament."

After coffee, the three officers returned to the bridge to join the double-watch on look out for aircraft. Seven o'clock came and passed; then 8 a.m. They were clearly visible from the air with either side liable to drop bombs.

At 8.50 a.m. a look-out shouted: "Aircraft on port quarter, sir, up sun, elevation 30 degrees." All eyes swivelled round to gaze intently towards the yellow ball of the rising sun. There it was, just a tiny black speck. The next few moments were filled with anxiety as the speck came closer but refused to alter course.

Suddenly it was recognizable as a Catalina and, by its position, could only be the one sent out by Fawkes to look for them. A breath of relief sighed through the submarine. Jewell waited until he judged the moment right and ordered: "Release a flare."

Instantly, the flare began to splutter as it gave off a brilliant green light and spat pieces of hot ash over the bridge. Would the Catalina see it?

"Release another," Jewell ordered quietly and now *Seraph* was bathed in brilliant green with Wright and Gaylord ducking to avoid the sudden squirts of flame.

Suddenly the aircraft dipped its wings in right turn and came towards *Seraph*, one of the airmen signalling the challenge of the day.

"Answer him," Jewell ordered, but just as the signalman aimed his lamp and pressed the trigger there was a splutter and the bulb burnt out. By now there was a chance that the aircraft, on getting no reply to his challenge, would drop his bombs. Excitement on the bridge mounted as the signalman dashed below for another bulb, returned to the conning tower and tried again. This time the Catalina came low and circled the submarine while a message was sent asking him to land and pick up passengers. He was also told to inform Gibraltar by radio of *Seraph*'s faulty transmitter.

By the time he got down and headed into the wind about 400 yards away, the Commandos had the canoes ready to make the transfer. Giraud and his party were brought up on deck and stood on the fore deck waiting for Wright and Gaylord to say goodbye to Jewell. Suddenly there was a shout from another look-out: "Aircraft dead astern coming this way. Elevation 10 degrees distance about 8,000 yards." It was coming in low—

about 200 feet—and fast. The look-out shouted again: "Looks like Ju. 88, sir."

They presented a perfect target—a Catalina squatting like a fat duck on the surface with a submarine almost alongside it. Jewell gave his orders rapidly and the decks were cleared, the Frenchmen being literally thrown down the conning tower hatch. The plane was almost near enough to drop its bombs when, without explanation, it swerved and Jewell, still half through the "lid", saw the split twin-tails of a Hudson. Reversing his orders, he climbed back to the conning tower with the crew and passengers following while the Hudson went into a wide circling patrol round them, obviously under orders to keep a watchful eye on their safety.

Then came the ludicrous operation of transferring the passengers to the aircraft, described in Jewell's official report.

"It is observed that the whole operation of transferring the passengers would have been greatly expedited had the aircraft stopped engines in the first place. *Seraph* had to turn to the wind and sea to create a lee for launching the folbots, but the aircraft proceeded at about one knot into the wind slowly widening the gap between aircraft and submarine. Furthermore, the draught caused by the propellers of the aircraft made it most difficult for the folbots to approach it.

"Then, when the aircraft did stop its engines eventually, a sea anchor would have been of the greatest assistance in the operation as with engines stopped the aircraft drifted to leeward nearly as fast as the folbots could proceed through the water so that they could get no closer despite strenuous efforts."

However, after frantic signals and shouting between *Seraph*, the aircraft and the folbots, all arrived safely and vanished into the Catalina's bulging belly. The commandos brought back the folbots and gathered round Jewell on the bridge to join him in waving at the aircraft which had begun to surge along the surface. Then it was in the air and for the first time in nearly two weeks they could relax. Giraud was on his way to join the high councils of war being held on the Rock with the large, bearded Wright to escort him into the presence of the men who wanted him most—Generals Eisenhower and Clark. *Seraph* was in at least friendly waters and would be home alongside *Maidstone* by nightfall the next day when, at the same time, the first invasion barges would be approaching the beaches of Algiers, Oran and Casablanca.

That night they were a changed crew. Days and nights of tension drained away and the first carefree laughter sounded from below as Jewell relaxed on the bridge with his officers. The Stars and Stripes had been hauled down and *Seraph* reverted to His Majesty's Navy.

Meanwhile, their sister, *Sybil*, was approaching the rendezvous point off La Fosette to meet the shoreboat with the ten members of Giraud's staff. With *Seraph* silent, Lieutenant Turner was uncertain of her whereabouts and kept an extra look-out in case of ramming or interfering with another operation. It was fifteen minutes after midnight and from the bridge he could see cars driving along the coast road and several trains on the Marseilles-Nice railway line. He made a mental note to return some day, when nothing else was on his mind, to use his gun on the railway.

In his report, Turner wrote: "At 0200 a small boat was seen pulling off from the shore and as it approached the submarine we could see it was painted white. Codeword for the operation had been given as 'Neptune', so after exchanging letters 'K' on dimmed lamps, I hailed the boat with: 'Neptune ahoy.' I was surprised to get a reply in a female voice saying softly through the darkness:

> 'They seek him here, they seek him there,
> Those Frenchies seek him everywhere,
> Is he in Heaven—is he in Hell?
> That demned elusive Pimpernel!' "

The shock of an unlisted woman passenger quoting the Scarlet Pimpernel at him at night only 300 yards off the enemy beach nearly caused Turner to turn *Sybil* about and steam off to seaward in the firm conviction that he had suffered a nightmare. Somehow, he overcame his natural inclination to run away and allowed the white-painted fishing boat to come alongside. The owner of the voice appeared from the shadows to reveal herself as an attractive young Englishwoman who introduced her three companions as members of Giraud's staff. She then asked Turner to wait while the fishing boat returned to the beach to pick up three more passengers and their baggage.

While they waited, she gave Turner some details about herself. She was the daughter of Lieutenant-Colonel Sir Broderick Hartwell and now married to Captain Beaufré, Giraud's chief of staff, who had left two nights before with the General in an "American" submarine. She was surprised that *Sybil* was British. She had been living in Algiers with her husband when war broke out and had driven a lorry in the front line. After the collapse of France, she had joined the Red Cross and driven supplies and medical equipment to prisoner of war camps. At the same time, her husband had been one of the leaders of the Resistance in Vichy France. Outspoken in his patriotism, he had been arrested several times by the Vichy Government. Now they were both in danger and had taken Giraud's advice to leave France with him and serve the Allies better in some safer area of operations.

Half an hour later the remainder of the party were aboard and *Sybil* headed out to sea, but three were missing. Turner's report says:

"These three failed to turn up and were thought to be in the hands of the police at Marseilles. The Marseilles headquarters of the Resistance had been raided for the second time in two days that morning and it was believed the three had been there collecting messages.

"Our passengers had spent an hour getting back from their 'safe' house at Cap d'Antibes to Le Lavendou and another hour getting from the Crois de Cagues railway station to the rendezvous, spending most of the time in the woods hiding behind trees.

"They were extremely thankful to see us and informed me we had made the rendezvous exactly in front of their house on the front. The lady passenger was invited to join our Wardroom mess where she used my bunk as a bedroom. She proved to be an excellent messmate with a good sense of humour. But when we landed her on the 11th at Algiers, she remarked on leaving the submarine: 'I left Algiers long ago with my head bowed and feeling very low, but now I have returned to help carry the torch towards victory.' "

Seraph entered Gibraltar on the 10th, tied up alongside *Maidstone* and the first aboard was Captain Fawkes. He had heard the story of OPERATION KINGPIN from Jerry Wright and Brad Gaylord. Now he mustered the crew and told them how well they had done their job. Later he took Jewell back to his cabin in *Maidstone* and they discussed the report to the Commander-in-Chief with the covering comment:

"This patrol is, I think, unique in that a United States naval officer (Captain Wright) was placed in nominal command of a British submarine in order that the distinguished passenger's request to be brought off by an American submarine might be acceded to. Captain Wright had accompanied P-219 on her previous successful mission, so his command was by no means strange to him."

Sir Andrew Cunningham added: "Lieutenant Jewell (and Captain Wright, U.S.N.) performed this delicate and important mission with judgment and efficiency."

For two weeks, *Seraph* lay resting alongside the depot ship, enjoying the attention showered on her by the repair crews. It was almost with reluctance that she limbered up again for her next voyage—this time a war patrol with the object of sinking enemy ships.

CHAPTER SEVEN

SERAPH DRAWS BLOOD

SERAPH sailed on her fourth Mediterranean voyage and first operational war patrol at 4 a.m. on November 24th. After an uneventful two days on passage she reached her operating area about eighty miles north of the Algerian port of Bone where it was hoped she might intercept enemy traffic to the island of Galita then occupied by German and Italian forces.

Two more days passed without incident and *Seraph* would have settled for just a peep at a whale to relieve the monotony. A signal was at last received from Captain Fawkes ordering her to move over to patrol across the Cagliari-Tunis route being used by the Axis to feed troops and supplies into Tunisia, the only German foothold in North Africa garrisoned by Von Arnim's recently arrived army and on which Rommel was falling back with the Eighth Army on his heels.

Seraph's hopes soared as she took up her new patrol—this was the Oxford Street of the Mediterranean, teeming with traffic and targets. There was not long to wait.

At 9.47 p.m. on the 29th, traffic lights changed to green and the first Axis supply ships to steam into her sector hove into sight—two fat, darkened shapes clearly silhouetted from *Seraph*'s bridge. A careful search of the shadows through binoculars showed there was not an escort in sight. Swiftly, she moved along her side street towards the main road and the interception point. On the bridge Jewell and Edsell kept their eyes on the targets while the two look-outs behind them swept the horizon astern to give warning of the approach of unexpected warships. The attack team in the control room plotted the information shouted down by Jewell and stood ready to swing into action once the firing point had been reached.

Seraph answered the helm readily as Jewell conned her to within 5,000 yards of the two ships, both beam on and presenting an elongated overlapping target. Now was the moment.

"Fire Numbers One, Two and Three. . . ."

Bolton pressed three levers in the control room, firing lights flashed in the for'ard torpedo room and the torpedoes hurtled from their tubes in the bows.

"Hard a'port. . . . Midships. . . . Steady. . . ."

The orders were shouted down from the bridge as *Seraph* came round and steadied on a new course. Every ear was waiting for the explosions which would signal their torpedoes had struck home. Only the crisp lap of water down *Seraph*'s sides and the throb of engines disturbed the stillness. The enemy were holding their course unaware of danger.

One minute and 35 seconds later a dull roar reverberated through the submarine and from the bridge the targets were starkly illuminated by a pillar of flame and smoke. One torpedo at least had run true. A faint cheer echoed through *Seraph*, but smiles left the faces of the bridge crew when the ship belched another flash followed by a vicious-sounding crack. To *Seraph* that was ominous; it sounded like a gun being fired and she had no wish to be winged at this stage of the proceedings.

Jewell pressed the alarm klaxon and fell down the conning tower hatch on Edsell's shoulder, slamming the "lid" shut above him. Spender muttered orders at the fore and after plane operators and steadied *Seraph* at periscope depth. Jewell bent down at the well and ordered: "Up periscope."

He caught the eyepieces low and straightened with the rise of the column. As the lens broke surface, water drained away and through the thin film of oil he saw as picturesque a sight as *Seraph* had ever witnessed. The target had not been firing at them as he had thought; instead it had become a glorious pyrotechnic of colour with streaks of flame careening about the sky. Obviously they had hit an enemy ammunition ship—he guessed its size as 3,000 tons.

While he was still peering through the periscope a flash caught his eye further to the left of the stricken merchantman; it was another torpedo striking the second ship. The thud of the impact reached *Seraph* seconds later, the shock raising her bows a little, but this 2,000-tonner merely toppled over and vanished from sight.

"Down periscope. We'll surface now." Turning to Spender, Jewell chuckled: "Not a bad night's work, Number One. We've taken our first bite from the Axis flank."

Looking from the bridge again across the still dark water, they watched the death agonies of the ammunition ship, the sounds of hot metal hissing in the water coming faintly across the sea as she sank lower before finally standing on her stern and sliding backwards to the bottom.

Seraph's bows nodded in the slight swell and she set off in search of fresh excitement while her batteries were charged for the coming daylight patrol, submerged. With two kills confirmed, she reloaded torpedo tubes in readiness for the enemy to put in another appearance.

For the next three hours she stalked her way through the blue-black night hidden from sight in the shadows of passing clouds. If she was invisible to the enemy, then they were equally lost to her. She saw nothing, which was just as well as it left the business of charging batteries uninterrupted.

Well-charged batteries are the vital key to the submarine's safety when submerged. A violent gale raging on the surface might have forced her to stay dived for an unusually long time: or it might have been a pitched battle overhead that would make it even more important to have plenty of electric current in hand. Enemy planes, destroyers, E-boats and an assorted variety of anti-submarine vessels could be agonisingly persistent when hunting their prey and might be expected to hover above her for more than twenty-four hours, keeping her continuously on the move and unable to surface.

The remainder of the night passed without disturbance and, just before dawn, *Seraph* dived to avoid the prying eyes of inquisitive aircraft of which the clear, bright blue sky was seldom empty. For a few seconds at frequent intervals her periscope poked up and swivelled round in a full circle as officers on watch searched for the enemy. But the thunderous action of the night before must have driven him into the side roads off "Oxford Street" to seek a safer passage out of range of *Seraph*'s deadly bite. He left the main road empty that day.

After dusk, she surfaced again, shook the water clear of her lean, cigar-like figure and set course for the Sicilian coast. Warm tropical air poured through her lungs and the pleasant aroma of breakfast spread from the galley where the cook was serving fried eggs to the crew who had tumbled blinking and yawning from their bunks. Overhead, brilliant stars and a yellow moon looked down on their reflections in the mirror-smooth sea.

Jewell, dressed like the crew in the traditional submariner's roll-necked sweater, scrambled up to the bridge to join Bolton. There, while unceasingly watching the horizon through swinging binoculars, they talked of the new suspected enemy minefields the navigator had recently marked on the charts.

At midnight the watch changed, Edsell relieved Bolton and saying good night to them both, Jewell went below to lie fully-dressed on his bunk. Little more than four hours later while the First Lieutenant was on watch, the alarm klaxon summoned the crew to action stations and sea-water cascaded on Spender's head as he fell down the hatch. He trimmed the submarine at periscope depth and was already at the eyepieces when Jewell charged into the control room, slapped him on the back and took over. Trapped in the periscope sights were two Italian Centaur class destroyers sweeping down "Oxford Street" on an asdic hunt for the submarine which had sent their shipping scurrying down back-alleys.

Destroyers, implacable enemies of submarines, made tempting targets, but *Seraph* was hunting more economically important game—fully-laden supply ships filled with the enemy's means of waging war. These were the losses which were hard to bear. It seemed likely to Jewell that such welcome sights would appear behind the destroyers and he sheered out of the way and waited to pounce when the expected convoy came in sight but, after the coming and going of the destroyers, the night was silent again.

Jewell cursed softly. He had allowed the enemy unmolested passage in the hope of more profitable kills and as a result had achieved nothing. Disgustedly, he allowed Spender to take *Seraph* to the surface while the crew relaxed, smoked their last cigarettes and ate supper before dawn broke and sent them down again.

At 8 a.m. two more destroyers were sighted through the periscope. They were astern and beyond reach: *Seraph* gazed at them with the soulful look of a small boy clutching a penny in a grubby hand and contemplating sweets which cost sixpence. A signal was received from Captain Fawkes which gave promise of better things that night. An important convoy was expected

General Giraud broadcasting to troops in North Africa.

Seraph returns to Algiers and Lieutenant Jewell (*left*) shares a joke with his First Lieutenant, Lieutenant W. D. Scott, as they tie up alongside *Maidstone*. Ferdinand the Bull is painted in front of the conning tower.

to pass near *Seraph*'s patrol area during the night and she was ordered to adjust her position to intercept.

The patrol was mostly composed of long periods of monotonous routine briefly punctuated by spells of wildly hectic action. It seemed there was no happy medium between the extremes. They looked forward now to the prospect of meeting the enemy again.

Captain Fawkes's intelligence had been remarkably accurate. *Seraph* surfaced at nightfall and began searching. At 9.06 p.m., according to Jewell's official Report of Proceedings, the enemy convoy came in sight. The crew could be forgiven if for a brief moment they wondered whether Guy Fawkes night was also an Italian anniversary; for it was not the convoy they sighted first but a full-scale air-sea battle which preceded the ships over the horizon.

Seraph, up ahead and almost in the path of the ships, sat back and watched with delight and admiration. It was a heavy concentration of bombers and the destroyer escorts were dashing hither and thither firing with every gun as they fought to protect their charges.

Each fresh attack from the air was heralded by the dropping of hundreds of flares which turned night into day. Jewell called his officers up to the bridge and, when the buzz had whipped round that there was "something worth seeing topsides", all those not yet at action stations poked their heads out.

The convoy then moved into the zone which had been designated at Allied Headquarters as a total bombing restriction area, meaning that our submarines were patrolling in those waters and had enough to deal with without being attacked by Allied aircraft. The bombers thoughtfully ceased dropping their loads and kept up a steady rain of flares instead, illuminating the scene of smoke and fire for any submarine in the vicinity. *Seraph* was there and she moved over towards a firing position.

The enemy had seen this ruse work before and realised immediately that he would soon come under torpedo attack. Six destroyers and three E-boats circled the convoy of six merchant ships at full speed laying a thick smoke screen between it and any investigating submarine. Fortunately, the screen was patchy on *Seraph*'s side and Jewell was able to point her nose on two large overlapping targets. Then her good fortune evaporated. One bomber dropped his barrage of flares short of the target and it hovered starkly over *Seraph* exposing her nakedly to the sight of the angry escorts. She was momentarily blinded; but not so the destroyers. Two of them made a tight, fast turn and, with bow waves curling high down their sides, came racing through the smoke to attack.

Jewell's thumb automatically pressed the klaxon and his last glimpse of the battlefield focussed on the destroyers as he leapt down the hatch and, with both feet planted firmly on the head of the look-out who had tumbled through first, slammed the "lid" tightly shut. *Seraph* was already submerging fast and had reached 60 feet when she started to tremble as the sound of tremendous roaring came from overhead. It was the two destroyers passing down either side, their fast-revving propellers kicking up a din faintly resembling an express train streaking through a tunnel. This was followed by a new noise—the rushing, clattering noise of dust bins caught up in a high wind. Depth charges!

There was nothing to do but wait with sinking stomachs for the explosions. When they came the world collapsed around them. At split-second intervals the roaring thunderclaps, known to submariners as "tonks", pounded *Seraph*'s tough young hull, throwing her around and sending the crew hurtling about the deck. Lights went out and came on again; everything movable skidded about and rolled to a stop; men pulled themselves upright at their action stations, and only the distant sound of propellers conducted through the water broke the silence.

It was over at last. *Seraph* had survived her baptism of the most dreaded form of attack. Her electric motors hummed evenly and, as Jewell altered course after the convoy, she shuddered slightly.

During a lull which Jewell took to be a break in the inferno upstairs, they broke surface again to see what had happened during their enforced absence. The convoy had now been attacked by the Inshore Squadron of cruisers and destroyers—first by air, then by submarine and now by surface units; the Germans were having a nasty time. But the battle had moved out of reach and *Seraph* was considering her next move when a look-out shouted excitedly:

"Darkened ships astern, sir."

It was nearly midnight, so *Seraph* turned about into the out-field for an inspection of the new arrivals. It seemed evident that they were either a slower part of the same convoy or a different one trying to slip through under cover of the battle ahead.

Seraph moved closer until Jewell made out the shapes of two leading transports of about 2,000 tons each. Forcing himself to take plenty of time, he manœuvred into the attack transmitting the enemy's course and speed to Edsell at the "fruit machine" who then passed torpedo settings to Bolton at the firing levers. *Seraph* was in position and Jewell ready to shout his firing orders when the earlier disasters repeated themselves.

A homeward-bound bomber flying low spotted the second convoy and dropped his flares wide of the targets. They burst into a brilliant glare right above *Seraph* who for the second time that night stood revealed in her naked glory. Two destroyers and a pair of E-boats raced towards her with guns pumping tracer bullets in her general direction.

Jewell's orders rang out over the sound of gunfire and whining bullets.

"Steady as you go, coxswain. . . .

"Stand by Numbers One, Two and Three. . . .

"Fire. . . ."

Seraph recoiled slightly as the 22-feet long steel pencils shot from her bows towards the target. Then the bridge crew were down the hatch, and the diving alarm klaxon began to shriek.

Orders in the control room were given softly but clearly and the attack team, working with precision smoothness, took her down and away from the immediate danger of being rammed. Closed up at action stations, the crew stood rigidly waiting for the next bombardment from above. At 100 feet Spender held her at "stopped trim"—that finely-balanced point at which the submarine is neither bodily heavy and liable to sink deeper nor bodily light and tending to rise towards the surface. Engines were stopped and all generators shut off. The crew were forbidden to whisper, for the slightest sound, the tread of a foot or the gurgle of water in a tank could be picked up by the enemy's asdic sets.

The lively *Seraph* had become an inert mass suspended between seabed and surface by the expert trimming of the First Lieutenant. Silent and alone, she waited for the attack from above. The depth charges would not have to hit her now: if they dropped near enough to upset that delicate balance, she would topple over like a stopped and balanced trick cyclist in a gust of wind.

Soundless, she lay in the cradle of the guillotine as seconds ticked by.

The seconds became minutes; disbelieving eyes glanced at watches; heads cocked upwards to hear better the passage of ships hunting on the surface. But why should they have to strain to hear if the hunters were above? They looked at each other for confirmation of the slowly-dawning truth. The enemy had moved away. Outwitted by the "silent routine", he had followed false trails; and, as though to prove the pendulum had swung back, *Seraph* trembled ever so slightly in the shock waves of depth charges dropped 400 yards away. She came alive as electricity pulsed into her engines and generators bringing movement and light. Carefully, she edged away from the depth charges towards safety. She had been stopped for five hours.

Despite the nearness of dawn, Jewell was determined to see what had happened to his torpedoes. He took *Seraph* to the surface and the bridge crew leapt to the conning tower to scan the sea for wreckage. And there it was, a large troop transport heavily afire and breaking up with loud cracks as girders split apart and fell into the sea in steaming clouds.[1]

The sea around was littered with dead bodies and wreckage; while the stench of oil through which they had come filled nostrils and penetrated every part of the submarine.

A mile away, thick columns of black smoke poured from a second ship, also burning fiercely.[2] Nothing else was in sight and Jewell, one eye on the paling light of approaching dawn, decided to dive and wait at periscope depth for the ships to sink.

[1] This was the 2,422-ton armed merchant ship *Puccini*.

[2] The Italian destroyer, *Folgore*, which with the *Puccini* was later sunk by the gunfire of the Inshore Squadron.

At 8.30 a.m. the periscope poked up and focussed on ten Carley rafts filled with survivors. Jewell noted in his report later: "It is of interest that all these survivors were wearing red cotton jackets and the rafts were painted a light dun—presumably these colours can be easily seen against the blue of the sea by rescue forces."

At 10 a.m. five destroyers appeared on the scene escorting a hospital ship and at once fanned out in a search for survivors. *Seraph*, weary but content with her night's work, discreetly withdrew to resume her patrol.

A brief report of the action was signalled to Captain Fawkes on the afternoon of the 3rd and in reply *Seraph* was ordered to take up a new patrol in the approaches to Naples. She arrived in this area at 7 a.m. on the 4th and almost immediately smoke was sighted through the periscope to the southeast. She moved over to intercept and an hour later picked out a hospital ship, a transport of about 5,000 tons and two destroyers. They were steaming at about 15 knots and only 3,000 yards away.

All torpedo tubes had been loaded while on passage to the area, and now the attack team closed up in the control room as Jewell hunched over the eyepieces preparing for the fourth action of the patrol. The hospital ship bothered him as it was too close to the transport and he could not make up his mind whether to chance hitting her or not. The enemy decided matters for him by altering course slightly and exposing a wide gap between the target and hospital ship.

Seraph's bows swung slightly and Spender adjusted the trim. At 9.18 a.m. exactly, six torpedoes shot from the tubes at ten-second intervals. Two minutes and thirty seconds passed before they heard the satisfying impact of a torpedo striking home. The periscope was raised and Jewell saw smoke pouring from the transport. He swung the periscope round in time to catch sight of a destroyer's bows nearly on top of them. At his urgent orders, *Seraph* was sent plummeting down to steady again at 100 feet, the ears of the crew still filled with the frightening roar of the thrashing propellers which had passed directly overhead and shaved the conning tower. It had been close indeed—too close.

This time there were no depth charges and *Seraph* made her way round to the other side of the convoy before again rising to periscope depth for Jewell to take a quick look at what was happening. There was no sign of the transport, nor of the destroyers, but he was near enough to see the name painted on the hospital ship, *S.S. Acquiligia,* which was stopped picking up survivors.

Seraph turned about and the duty watch took her back to resume patrolling. In the afternoon another convoy of two supply ships passed close by escorted by a destroyer and two E-boats. She fired her only remaining torpedo and, to the disappointment of his crew who had come to think him a crack shot, Jewell missed. The attack team felt too bitter even for the solace of profanity.

However, *Seraph* had stirred up more than a little turmoil in the area and it was quite clear to the enemy that a British submarine was somewhere in the neighbourhood. They reacted logically and took appropriate measures. *Seraph* made her way slowly towards safer pastures, and when she surfaced that night two destroyers were hunting a few miles away, sweeping the sea with powerful searchlights. With nothing but a 3-inch gun and the machine-guns left, it was not likely that she could put up much of a show. So she prudently made off at full speed for home which, according to recent signals, had been switched from Gibraltar to Algiers.

Over breakfast that evening the officers mused on the possibility of again meeting the American members of their Wardroom Mess.

CHAPTER EIGHT

THE CANOEISTS CLUB

W HILE *Seraph* had been on patrol, events in North Africa had moved swiftly and surely to a climax. The Algerian ports had fallen to Allied troops—most of the defences having been handed over intact by the French as a result of General Clark's meeting with General Mast—and the two German-Italian armies under Von Arnim and Rommel were being squeezed into the Tunisian "pocket" by the Anglo-American invasion forces to the west, and the Eighth Army to the east in the desert.

Now the Eighth Submarine Flotilla was moved to Algiers from where it would operate against the supply routes from Italy and Sicily to the North African coast. Having crossed the Mediterranean, enemy ships hugged the African shore until they reached their unloading ports. In these shallow waters and protected by shore guns, aircraft and coastal escorts, they were not ideal targets; yet the "S" class submarines under Captain Fawkes achieved some of their most remarkable successes under these conditions.

Maidstone had sailed to Algiers and, on December 8th, *Seraph* arrived on the surface at the harbour entrance. A signal from *Maidstone* ordered her to lay off until met by a messenger being sent in the depot ship's launch. The crew speculated about this odd order while the motor-boat rounded a promontory and headed for *Seraph*. In a few minutes it arrived alongside and a sub-lieutenant handed a parcel to a member of the crew on the foredeck and called out to Jewell:

"With the compliments of Captain Fawkes, sir. He says you are to open the parcel before entering harbour." Then he waved and the launch turned back. Jewell waved in reply; he could guess what it was—likewise the grinning crew. He took the parcel from the crewman and glanced at the address. It was simply marked "J.R."

"This is it, Number One. Have it hoisted," and he tossed it across the bridge to Spender who unwrapped the paper and held out a large black flag with a huge skull and crossbones painted in white in the middle. It was the flotilla commander's traditional acknowledgement of a submarine's success. No submarine was entitled to fly the Jolly Roger unless it had been given by the captain of her flotilla; thereafter it became the property of the submarine and could be flown on entering harbour only after a successful patrol. It was hoisted until sunset on the day of arrival and not again until another victorious return.

As the Jolly Roger fluttered stiffly from the mast abaft the bridge, they felt proud and happy. *Seraph* had been blooded.

Maidstone was mother and father to the submarines of the Eighth Flotilla and the crew rushed to enjoy the luxuries she offered. They bathed for the first time in two weeks; shaved and felt the crisp coolness of freshly-laundered clothes against their scrubbed bodies; messed with the depot personnel of their respective ranks; saw films in the evening and at "lights out" slipped between clean blankets to sleep with both eyes shut and without fear of being summoned to action stations.

Jewell handed in his Report of Proceedings to Captain Fawkes who that same night sent an analysis to the Commander-in-Chief, Sir Andrew Cunningham, with his own comment: "This patrol reflects great credit on the Commanding Officer and ship's company and follows closely on three patrols in two of which most important missions were carried out with skill and determination."

On forwarding this to the Admiralty, Sir Andrew added: "This successful and fruitful patrol was most efficiently conducted and augurs well for Lieutenant Jewell and the people of P.219."

That night Jewell and his officers relaxed in *Maidstone* sipping drinks and keeping very much to themselves. They were still wound up like dynamos, and their minds still held the sight of a sea festooned with bodies, while in their nostrils lingered the grim smell of oil and salt water carrying with it the stench of death.

The next morning brought a pleasant surprise. Across the gangway stalked the tall, thick-set figure of her second commanding officer, Captain Wright. She had not seen him for some weeks, but he had kept in touch with her movements by badgering Captain Fawkes for information whenever close enough to call in person or by telephone.

His friendly voice shouted greetings as he clambered down to the Wardroom and Jewell stood up to welcome him.

"Come to take over your command, sir ?" he asked smilingly.

"No, Bill, not this time. I'm here just to look her over and see you're taking good care of her."

Wright shook hands with the officers whose christian names he had remembered faultlessly, and asked for a glass of gin.

"General Clark's here, you know, Bill," he said quietly, "and when he heard *Seraph* was coming in yesterday he told me he would like to stage a re-union of our North African Canoeists Club. He's planning to throw a dinner tonight."

"That sounds a lot of fun. Where are the rest of the founder members ?"

"Our side is all here. Lemnitzer, Julius Holmes, Arch Hamblen and Brad Gaylord. If you bring your boys, all we need are those three Commando brigands to bring us to full strength."

Arrangements were made for a U.S. Army jeep to pick up *Seraph's* officers in the evening, then Wright and Jewell boarded *Maidstone* to lunch in the Wardroom and find out where Courtney, Livingstone and Foote might be. After lunch a messenger arrived with the news that they were engaged on a small raiding party in Corsica where a partisan leader had been captured by the Italians. Their mission was to release him and bring him back to Allied headquarters in Algiers.

In the evening the N.A.C. Club, membership of which was strictly limited to those who had taken part in Operations Flagpole and Kingpin, met at the Hotel de France run at that time by an energetic and extremely capable Frenchwoman. Mark Clark, who for many days had been swimming against the tide in a sea of French politics trying to resolve differences between Darlan, Giraud and a host of minor leaders in North Africa, was obviously delighted at this opportunity to meet old friends and talk of military and naval adventures with which he was more intimately familiar.

The five Americans and four *Seraph* officers—two had stayed aboard to deal with emergencies—relived the missions

to North Africa and France. This "shop talk" gave the propriet-
ress time to produce a meal which even in those days of scarcity
in Algiers was in keeping with the best traditions of French
cooking.

The Club members ate well, drank well and laughed louder,
especially when Clark suddenly announced:

"What d'you know, boys? Remember I lost my pants and
we started the priority pants racket? Well, when I got back to
London, I had a message that my pants had been washed up on
the beach and found by our friends at the white house. And
when I first arrived here the French handed me back the pants
all dry-cleaned and pressed. They came to just below my
knees."

The roars of laughter quickly subsided when he told them
how successful "Flagpole" had been. For the first time they
heard the full story of what had happened ashore; the result
being that in many parts of Africa Allied troops had been able
to take over key strongpoints and vital communication centres
with little or no resistance.

"I told you at Gib. that I hoped the conference would save
lots of lives. Well, you can take it from me it saved thousands,
and you chaps carry just as much of the responsibility for it as
we do. On behalf of my countrymen, I want to say, thanks a lot."

It was the nearest thing to a speech during the evening and
as it was not the time or place for Deputy Supreme Commanders
and staff officers to stay out too late at nights, Clark announced
the end of the first re-union dinner. Before they left the hotel,
he asked Jewell if he might visit *Seraph* the following day to
"say hullo to some of the boys".

The next afternoon a number of the crew had gone ashore
and a repair party from *Maidstone* was working on the submarine's deck casing. About 3 p.m. General Clark arrived on
board unannounced, accompanied by Lemnitzer. Before going
below to see Jewell and the officers, they walked along the deck
to greet the crew. Solemnly, the senior American officers shook
hands with each man they met saying; "Mighty glad to see you
again, sailor. Just want to say thank you for what you did for
us. Didn't have much time when we left the boat."

Keen-eyed Lemnitzer was the first to become a little
uncomfortable at the bewildered look on the faces of the first

few sailors who came rigidly to attention and only shook hands with the greatest reluctance. He glanced round the deck and recognised one familiar face screwed up with suppressed laughter. It was Leading Mechanic Hinds. Lemnitzer walked over to him, shook his hand and said: "What's so funny?"

"Well, sir. I didn't know what you were doing at first, otherwise I would have tipped you off. But those chaps you and General Clark are talking to don't belong to *Seraph*, sir. They're a repair party from *Maidstone*, sir."

Lemnitzer stared at him incredulously and then with a chuckle crossed the deck and whispered to Clark. They followed Hinds down the fore hatch ladder and repeated the hand-shaking process with their old shipmates.

When they reached the Wardroom, Lemnitzer announced jovially to Jewell: "Been showing the General round the U.S.S. *Seraph*, Bill. We met a few of the boys and said hullo. Good sailors, but they'd look better in our uniform."

The cross-banter went on while *Seraph*'s officers entertained their guests until the time came to leave. On deck they were greeted by an astonishing sight. All the sailors were working normally, but somehow they looked different. The American officers noticed the truth first and crossed the gangway in a burst of laughter, while Jewell and Spender who had come up to see their guests off stood speechless with surprise. All the crew were in the proper rig of the day except for caps. On the head of each was perched a white United States Navy cap shoved well back. And each face was contorted as it chewed real or imaginary gum.

Discipline in submarines was strict, but with it went a democratic spirit unknown in bigger ships which compensated for much of the hardship. It was a rare comradeship shared by all from the commanding officer down. Because of this, Jewell and Spender were able to return below to share the joke in the Wardroom.

It was discovered later that Lemnitzer's remark about the U.S.S. *Seraph* had been overheard by a sailor who knew that one of the *Maidstone* messes had come back from a spree ashore laden with American navy caps. He had rushed over with his mates, borrowed the caps and distributed them before Clark and Lemnitzer left.

That night Eisenhower invited Clark, Fawkes and Jewell to dine with him. In this way he created the opportunity to thank Jewell personally for his rôle in two secret missions.

Later Clark left Algiers for a tour of the front, and in *Maidstone*'s Wardroom someone remarked: "I wonder how long we shall have *Seraph* on strength. Someone's bound to ask for her soon to go on some crazy mixed-up mission—maybe, we'll be using whales against the Axis soon."

CHAPTER NINE

OPERATION PEASHOOTER

DURING December, the build-up of German troops and supplies in Tunisia was almost equal to that of the Allied forces in French North Africa. A continuous stream of ships sailed between Italy and Sicily at one end, and the ports of Bizerta and Tunis at the other. The 100 miles of sea between were protected by large flocks of Luftwaffe fighters.

Admiral Cunningham was determined to sever this sea link; in addition to submarines he threw a considerable number of assorted coastal forces into the battle. These were not as successful as he might have hoped since they rarely sighted the enemy in sufficient size to warrant attack. There could be only one possible reason for this—the enemy was receiving accurate intelligence concerning the movements of our ships.

Counter-intelligence investigation showed the most likely source of this activity to be Galita Island, eighty miles north of the African coast, which was often used by Allied surface ships and submarines as a navigational aid. It was known to be held by a small force of German and Italian troops who could be charting positions of our vessels and signalling to Italian Naval headquarters in either Tunis or Italy. The only way to make certain was to go and take a look.

On December 10th a significant conference took place at a small house on the coast near Bone—characteristic of Algierian houses it was painted white with a red-tiled roof—which was being used by Combined Operations as an advanced field headquarters. Present were Major Lord Jellicoe,[1] whose shadowy figure flitted in and out of many conferences where daring, unorthodox raids were planned; Captain Norman Vincent Dickinson, R.N.,[2] an intrepid beach-master who landed ahead of invading forces to direct their movements into perimeter defences; and Colonel William O. Darby[3] of the

[1] Now Lt.-Colonel and employed inside the Baghdad Pact organisation.
[2] Now Rear-Admiral (Retired).
[3] Killed in action during the Rhine crossing in 1944.

United States Rangers, whose reputation as a two-fisted fighting officer was second only to that of General Patton.

Their object: the reconnaissance of Galita's beaches, the securing of intelligence concerning the island's defences and the subsequent landing, if worthwhile, of a small raiding and occupying force comprising both Rangers and Commandos. Their decisions: Dickinson to carry out the reconnaissance, and Darby's Rangers and Jellicoe's Commandos to gather in Gibraltar and sail for Bone late in the month.

In the next few days, Captain Dickinson had to allow other operations to take first call on his landing-craft personnel. But, on the 16th, Lieutenant E. G. N. Mansfield, R.N., suggested he should be allowed to land on Galita, investigate its beaches and be taken off again. There were sufficient available officers to mount the trip, so Dickinson agreed, and arrangements were made for "Operation Peashooter"—code name for the reconnaissance and landing—to begin the following day. For security reasons, Dickinson wished to avoid taking ratings and eventually decided to use a specially armoured landing craft manned by officers only. Those chosen were, in addition to Dickinson and Mansfield, Lieutenant Van Cleef, R.N.V.R., Sub-Lieutenants P. R. Lawrence, R.N., and L. Malone, R.N.V.R.—the last-named acting as stoker to keep the engines running.

The landing craft sailed at 6.15 p.m. on the 17th, made the crossing to Galita in four uneventful hours and slowed to a stop three miles south of the island. It had been originally intended that Mansfield should be landed that night and embarked at the same time and place on the next.

According to Captain Dickinson's official report on the operation, "It was calm with a bright moon with some cloud. As it was shining brightly at the time we should have put Lieutenant Mansfield ashore I decided it would be impossible for us to pass between the island and the Sicilian mainland without being sighted. It seemed pointless—even foolhardy—under those conditions to land anyone."

Dickinson took the landing craft to within 400 yards of the shore and the team began mapping the beachline, hill contours and possible exits inland. They turned northwards up the east coast with a sudden slight overcast making their progress less easy to spot from the shore.

It was soon evident that a landing on the east coast was going to prove difficult and costly. No beach of any sort was seen and even if troops could have made a toehold on the rocky shore there were no satisfactory exits inland. They would have been simple targets for a mere handful of defenders. On the north side, however, the team charted some "narrow defiles and precipitous slopes which might have to be used as exits from the shore if the rest of the coast offers nothing".

On the run down the west side of the island, the landing craft was fewer than 100 yards from the cliffs and the moon had come out again from behind its occasional covering of cloud. Any idle glance seaward from ashore could hardly fail to spot them. It was comparatively easy to see that no suitable landing place for the raiders existed on the west coast. That left the southern side on which was Galita Bay, headquarters of the enemy force and used by his supply ships. Dickinson decided to have a look at what was in the Bay.

The landing craft rounded the western point shielding the Bay on which was perched a signal station. A light was shining from it and, across the few yards separating them, the team could see signs of activity. The moon was very bright—brighter than a searchlight to the stealthy men in a boat below. Rounding the point, the team scanned the harbour through binoculars expecting to see several small supply ships and a gunboat at least, but it was deserted except for a small coaster which appeared to be resting on the bottom.

There was still no sign of their having been seen by the signal station, so Dickinson decided to enter the Bay and attack the coaster, a decision which would take the landing craft to within feet—not yards—of the shore. Any one of the five officers could have been picked off in the moonlight by an average rifle shot.

At Mansfield's order a miscellany of hand grenades, sub-machine guns and homemade explosive bombs on the design of Molotov cocktails was magically produced and laid on the canvas cover of the boat, ready for instant use.

"I intended," said Dickinson in his report, "to lob the grenades and other explosives into the coaster as we passed alongside her and use the Lewis guns against her crew."

The landing craft was still 100 yards from the target and 50 yards from the nearest shore when they were discovered. A quick red flash came from a hidden gun emplacement and a shell screamed overhead to land somewhere on the opposite side of the island. Dickinson ordered full speed and turned about to head southwards with tracer bullets whistling around and above them. One of the party calmly noted that the "enemy appear to have six machine-gun posts and a heavy gun emplacement evenly spaced round the shore of the Bay".

While the boat was still turning away, Lieutenant Van Cleef at the helm had to keep sticking his head out of the steering cockpit to see where he was going.

"Only by doing this could he con the craft adequately," wrote Captain Dickinson. "During one such venturesome act a tracer bullet struck the edge of the cockpit and a splinter wounded him in the forehead. Although bleeding profusely and somewhat dazed he stayed at the wheel until we were clear of the Bay and the enemy's fire. Luckily his wound was superficial."

The party returned to Bone, fortunate that Van Cleef's injury was the only penalty for such an impudent invasion of enemy property.

Dickinson's report, sent to Lord Jellicoe and the Commander of the Inshore Naval Squadron, delayed "Peashooter" until a further conference on the 19th decided that a submarine might be able to operate for longer close inshore without detection and a detailed reconnaissance carried out, on which the future of the island would depend.

The next day Jewell was told to report to Captain Fawkes in *Maidstone*. When he arrived he was introduced to Lord Jellicoe, Captain Dickinson and Colonel Darby. The purpose of this briefing session was explained and Fawkes added that *Seraph* would sail the following morning taking Dickinson and Darby along as passengers. All further leave for the sailors was to stop and no one was to know the reason for the passengers' presence. "Operation Peashooter," said Fawkes, "is tied up by security. That island might yet be more important than we think."

Seraph's formal orders were delivered by hand with the prefix: "On no account are these orders to be allowed to fall into enemy hands and are to be destroyed by fire when complied

Torpedoes ready: for'ard communications rating between two torpedo tubes.

Landing craft towed in to Sicily for "Operation Husky".

Surfaced by day, *Seraph*'s gun crew on exercises.

H.M.S. *Maidstone*—"mother" to *Seraph* and a brood of seven other submarines which comprised the Eighth Submarine Flotilla.

(*below*) Officers on the bridge of a troop transport watch fighting ashore as landing craft are directed to the beaches by *Seraph*.

with." They opened by reminding the Commanding Officer that further information and intelligence would be supplied by Combined Operations Headquarters.

1. The enemy are now occupying the Island of Galita, they are known to possess a wireless transmitting and receiving set but it is not known if they have Radar. This island is believed to be a reporting station for the movements of our ships and aircraft.

2. It is intended that *Seraph* shall carry out a periscope reconnaissance of Galita to obtain information on the most suitable beaches on which to land a force from surface vessels to capture the island. The codeword for the operation is PEASHOOTER.

3. Your object is to give every facility to reconnaissance officers to inspect the beaches of Galita; to land these officers at Bone on completion; then to attack enemy war and merchant vessels.

4. For outward bound passage TOTAL BOMBING RESTRICTIONS have been arranged for the 21st and SUBMERGED bombing restrictions for ten miles on either side of your route from thirty-five miles ahead to fifty-five miles astern thereafter.

5. Throughout OPERATION PEASHOOTER our own forces have been instructed to stay clear of your operational area and you may sink on sight any vessel.

Seraph sailed from Algiers on the 21st and ran into one of the worst concentrations of enemy aircraft over the area since the outbreak of the North African war. Flares fell in layers for most of the night and Jewell, taking no chances with his passengers, travelled for the next thirty hours submerged at an average speed of three knots. David Scott had taken over as Number One from Spender, who had been transferred to another submarine.

Dickinson and Darby proved an amusing pair with a whole repertoire of new jokes and anecdotes. Darby, it seemed, was more than thankful to be hidden from the world in a submarine. In Algiers he had been staying with a French family who were not averse at times to sinking their fair share of alcohol. One evening, the American Colonel, already infused with the spirit of approaching Christmas, decided to brew his own punch. As he poured in the contents he sampled it at regular intervals

H

and, when the mixture was to his liking, invited the family to share it.

All was well until the family asked him to accompany them to midnight Mass to which he readily agreed. His next recollection was a powerful jab in the ribs from a stranger who said politely:

"If monsieur must snore, will monsieur please try to synchronise the sound with the Service."

He was anything but popular with his hosts on their return home and most thankful to leave next day for his rôle in "Peashooter".

Seraph surfaced off Galita at dawn on the 23rd and Dickinson at once settled down to the job of charting the beaches—this time in daylight. Again, the enemy noticed nothing while *Seraph* prowled round the east, north and west sides. Approaching the Bay, Darby noticed, through the periscope, a horse looking at them between mouthfuls of grass from a hill. The high-powered lens made the horse appear only a few feet away. For some reason it fascinated him and having brought his camera he settled down to take innumerable shots of the animal.

The reconnaissance lasted for eight hours and well into the afternoon before Dickinson decided he had all the information he needed. The men were relieved, for it was unnatural for submarines to gambol in enemy waters on the surface without being blown to pieces by shore batteries. It seemed only a matter of time before they would be sighted and under fire.

Thankfully, *Seraph* dived and was about to quit those dangerous waters when Colonel Darby pleaded for just another look at the beautiful island through the periscope. Jewell assented and, proudly, Darby called out in his best British accent: "Up periscope."

A poker-faced rating carried out the order and Darby glued himself to the eyepieces. A great beam of appreciation spread across his face. Then he muttered suddenly to no one in particular: "Hullo, I've found another gun. I can see soldiers running towards it. They're manning it. The barrel is swinging round towards us. Cripes . . . duck, you chaps, it's fired."

And he ducked so low he bumped the deck with his head. A gust of laughter swept the control room as he glanced up to see the crew lounging at their stations, and climbed sheepishly to his feet.

"Gee, I forgot where I was, boys."

Seraph, however, was taking no chances. She went down to 60 feet and crept slowly seawards out of range.

That evening, she surfaced for fresh air, cigarettes were lit and the usual clatter of pots and pans came from the galley where breakfast was already under way. The crew came on deck in pairs to enjoy the beauty of a Mediterranean night after the nerve-racking business of spending day within slingshot distance of the enemy.

During breakfast, Dickinson told Darby and Jewell his final findings concerning "Peashooter". It was a little difficult because both answered to the name, Bill.

"You know, Bill," he said, looking at Darby, "it's no use. A landing anywhere except in Galita Bay itself would be a waste of time. Even if landed, a large number of men would bog down on that shore through lack of exits from the beach. Because of the nature of the coastline—there are no real beaches —and what exits there are could be death traps, I say the whole idea of taking Galita is impracticable."

"You're right," Darby replied, "up to a point, I guess. If my boys were really trained the maximum I'd say a few of us, not more than 100, could take it easily, but with those beaches we might be cut to pieces with untrained troops. We'll be ready to tackle that lump of rock by about the end of the month according to the present training programme."

"No," said Dickinson, "There won't be much point then. From what I hear we shall bypass the thing entirely. It won't be much use once the Germans pack up in Tunisia."

Darby shrugged agreement and Jewell left them to continue their discussion on the fate of Galita while he joined Scott who had just taken the watch on the bridge.

Shortly after 8 p.m., Darby joined Jewell on the bridge and said flatly: "I think we can do it. Dammit, there's nothing the 1st United States Ranger Battalion can't handle." There was no time for Jewell to reply. The starboard look-out suddenly shouted:

"Darkened ship starboard beam, sir. Looks like a submarine."

With a curt order to Darby to get below quickly, Jewell swung his glasses round until they rested on the unmistakable shape of an enemy U-boat high on the surface. Movements and orders came with swift precision. The alarm klaxon called the men to action stations. "Hard a-starboard . . . midships . . . steady as she goes, coxswain." They pointed at the enemy lying dead ahead. It seemed impossible for her look-outs not to have spotted them. "Stand by Number One tube. . . . Blast, it's diving."

The U-boat had sighted *Seraph* swing round to the attack and was not waiting for a surface engagement. Cursing softly, Jewell watched her shadowy shape slip downwards and gave the order to dive.

Still pointing in the enemy's direction, *Seraph* went down to 120 feet and levelled off to allow the asdic operator to listen out for the U-boat's echo. He searched without result for a few minutes and then went up for another hunt at 60 feet. Suddenly, the crew were sent tumbling about in all directions as a tremendous crash sounded for'ard. No genius was needed to diagnose the trouble. *Seraph* had come up underneath the enemy and rammed him. Men were picking themselves up when the second loud thump sent them to the deck again. Sutton rushed to the bow compartment to see if there had been any damage. He had entered the torpedo room when the third—and worse—crash keeled *Seraph* over on her side at an alarming angle. The U-boat had passed over her upper deck.

Now the astonished and indignant *Seraph* was clear and with Jewell already tearing at the "lid" grips, she broke surface to meet the enemy with gun and torpedo fire.

Almost immediately, another look-out sighted two periscopes poking out of the water a few yards away on the starboard side. *Seraph* dived to periscope depth and turned towards the enemy again—loud hydrophone effect coming from the asdic speaker. Then it stopped and the operator scanned the depths for some sight of the enemy's presence. It was useless. Assuming the U-boat had gone deep on "silent routine", Jewell gave orders to surface again. *Seraph* turned her head away from the elusive enemy and resumed her voyage to Bone.

Down below, the two passengers were excitedly demanding to be given the story. When they were told, Dickinson muttered:

"What a pity we didn't get him. That would have been quite an experience for me. Not that after the last few minutes I want much more of submarine life."

Darby was also emphatic in his opinions of the Submarine Service. "Hell, if you boys go through this sort of thing as normal routine, just get me back to my Rangers quick. I don't feel at all safe in this baby."

Seraph ran along the surface charging her batteries for a while and after midnight dived to avoid being sighted by enemy aircraft. Before dawn she surfaced again to top up the batteries and for the rest of the daylight hours of the 24th stayed submerged.

She came up after dark and ran into immediate trouble. She had hardly settled down to her best clip on the diesel engines when the starboard look-out again gave warning: "Darkened shape off starboard bow, sir. Looks like an enemy submarine."

The attack team closed up in the control room, and Jewell rushed to the bridge in time to see the U-boat approaching close on an opposite course. This time the enemy was given no time to dive. Three torpedoes leapt from *Seraph*'s bows and from the bridge they could see the bubbles in the tracks. The first went dead straight—a perfect shot that never looked like missing. The other two went astray and a report came up from the control room that the ramming of the previous night had damaged the fore torpedo tubes. Suddenly they heard the distant thump of a torpedo striking home. Jewell wrote in his Report. "We could see the torpedo run straight at the target and hit below the conning tower amidships. But for some reason it failed to explode. I decided to go into gun action."

This was the cook's chance. As gunlayer during surface action, he swung the 3-inch in the general direction of the U-boat and peered through his telescopic eyepiece. For several seconds he strained to find the target. Eventually he gave up in exasperation and reported to the bridge: "Can't find the target, sir."

Jewell was not surprised. Scared out of his wits by the sudden impact of a torpedo, the enemy had almost certainly performed a 30-second vanishing trick of which even *Seraph* might have been proud. He was probably hundreds of feet below at that moment, mopping his brow and thanking the gods for a lucky escape.

But it was not for them to surmise. They had to find out, and down they went to scan the depths for some sign of submarine life. At 200 feet they were shocked to hear a dull, rumbling beneath them. *Seraph* shuddered in the shock waves. Then came three distinct cracks and it seemed possible that the enemy might be sinking and breaking up, but there was no evidence to support this hope, so they surfaced once again and headed for Bone.[1]

After this double experience of meeting U-boats, Dickinson and Darby were, as the Ranger Colonel put it, "Downright glad to see the last of *Seraph* for a while. Put me ashore, give me a gun and there isn't anyone or anything I won't face. But, gee, Bill, I haven't been so scared in my life as in the last two days. Thanks for the ride. I'll let someone else take it next time."

The two passengers were dropped at Bone and, it being Christmas Day, the cruiser *Arethusa*, which was taking supplies aboard in Bone, invited *Seraph* alongside to join in the seasonal festivities.

They swarmed aboard as guests of their respective messes. Jewell had Christmas lunch with Rear-Admiral Sir Cecil Harcourt while his officers dined in the Wardroom. Late in the evening, the crew rejoined their submarine and left Bone for Algiers and *Maidstone*.

On the way that night she was sighted by an enemy E-boat which opened fire with tracers. She dived out of harm's way and continued her passage. She tied up to *Maidstone* on the 28th and a thankful off-duty crew rushed to baths and clean clothes.

The Report of Proceedings for that trip was forwarded by Captain Fawkes to the Commander-in-Chief with a covering letter:

"*Seraph* had very bad luck in the second attack. Her snap attack was good and should have brought success. It is not possible to assume that the enemy was destroyed. It is likely,

---

[1] It was the Italian submarine, *Alagi*, which returned to base so badly damaged that she made no more operational trips during the war.

however, that both U-boats have been badly damaged and may be out of the battle for some time."

Another disappointment was awaiting Jewell. The day before, Sir Andrew Cunningham had informed Combined Operations and Captain Fawkes that no troops could be spared from the impending decisive battle in Tunisia to put Galita out of action. Therefore it had been decided to call off the landing and bypass the island.

Ramming the U-boat had damaged *Seraph* more seriously than had at first been thought. An inspection by the dockyard experts at Algiers showed her bows to be buckled, the torpedo tubes bent out of alignment and the bulkheads distorted. She would need to go home to England for repairs.

Seraph was not sorry. She had been on continuous operations for long enough to need a rest. The constant strain of sailing into enemy waters on missions so secret that the crew could not be told where they were going or why, punctuated by operational patrols and constant encounters with the enemy, were having their effect.

Two days after arriving in Algiers, the already bad-tempered relations between two leading hands who had once been friends broke into open conflict when one grabbed a large, evil-looking carving knife from the galley and tried to stab the other in the back. A fight broke out and a chase developed through the submarine. Only the timely intervention of a group of Petty Officers prevented a nasty murder and subsequent court-martial.

This was followed by an outbreak of one of the worst forms of crime in ships at sea—stealing. All the thefts were petty— a cigarette case, a few shillings, a fountain pen or a lighter— but the total added up to an epidemic which had to be stamped out.

With these worries on her mind, *Seraph* sailed for England on January 8th, 1943, for a well-earned overhaul. On the way through the Mediterranean she was attacked by a flight of Allied bombers and suffered several near misses. While a genuine mistake had undoubtedly been made by the pilots, *Seraph* reflected sadly that in her brief life she had come nearer to death at the hands of her friends than by enemy action.

The remainder of the trip home was eventful only for her

increasing apparent weariness. Sluggish of helm, unable to maintain her speed and riding lower in the water than normal, she limped painfully into Blyth on the 28th. The next day, she lay down in the dry-dock to recuperate while dockyard surgeons worked on her broken nose and overstrained body.

She had left England six months before, a mere child. Now she returned, honoured and fêted as a veteran fighter.

CHAPTER TEN

OPERATION MINCEMEAT

A T Blyth, the dockyard engineers diagnosed *Seraph* as being in need of new bows and torpedo tubes. They also decided to give her an oerlikon gun mounted on a specially erected platform abaft the conning tower. Although this additional armament was designed to increase her anti-aircraft fire power, it was also to add to the anxiety of the crew. In silhouette, she would now resemble an Italian U-boat—and this could prove embarrassingly complicated some dark night should friendly warships be patrolling in her vicinity.

While hordes of dockyard workers descended upon the *Seraph*, Jewell stayed with his father and mother at their home in Pinner, Middlesex. The *London Gazette* announced that he had been made an M.B.E. for his "skill, daring and cool judgment while executing special operations for the Supreme Allied Commander in North Africa". The Admiralty followed this with an official statement that the "special operations" had led to "the submarine *Seraph* becoming the spearhead of the Allied landings".

The Jewell home was immediately besieged by reporters and photographers demanding his personal account of the adventures which lay behind the brief official phrases. He had to refuse to say anything more than had been released and eventually went to ground with friends until the newspapers called off their hunt. To his delight he found among his fellow M.B.E.s the Commando trio—Courtney, Livingstone and Foote.

For his mission to North Africa, General Clark had received one of his country's highest awards, the Legion of Merit. Eisenhower also recommended Wright, Holmes, Hamblen, Lemnitzer and Jewell for awards suitable to their ranks.

Snags cropped up in the case of the two naval officers. Clark's recommendation concerning Wright was forwarded to the Chief of Naval Operations in Washington, Admiral King, who, determined to place on record that his officers were well cared for, stalked to the office of General Marshall, the Army Commander-in-Chief, and threw the message down with the comment: "Who the hell is Clark?" He knew perfectly well, but felt the Army should be given a reminder that he was capable of making his own recommendations for awards and promotion.

This was largely mock indignation, for on December 1st, Eisenhower had written to Admiral Harold Stark, chief of the United States Naval Forces in Europe, saying:

"I have a matter involving naval personnel which I want to present to you since I recall that Admiral King asked that this procedure be followed in such cases. It involves Captain Jerauld Wright, U.S.N.

"As you know, Captain Wright was detailed to the Allied Staff immediately after the TORCH concept. Since that time he has been constantly on duty with us and has rendered services that are literally invaluable. In addition to his fine staff work, his sound judgment and his unfailing readiness to help in any kind of job that arises, he has been on two missions in which he operated with signal success.

"The first of these was as a member of the Clark mission and the other was in command of the submarine which brought Giraud out of France.

"For all these reasons I should like very much to bring Captain Wright's name to the favourable attention of the Navy Department for whatever action Admiral King might deem appropriate. Were he an officer of the Army I should have already recommended him for promotion but since I am unfamiliar with Navy policies I feel the best solution is to bring all these things to your attention. . . ."

This was followed a few days later by a letter to Jerry Wright from the Supreme Commander who said:

"As Commander-in-Chief, Allied Force, I desire to express to you my appreciation and commendation of the able and skilful manner in which you developed and executed the exacting and difficult plan which enabled General Henri Giraud, French Army, to leave France by submarine for consultation with me and my staff in North Africa.

"The exemplary conduct, sound judgment and courage

which you demonstrated in accomplishing this important undertaking are in keeping with the finest traditions of the United States Navy."

The result of this was that, in March, Wright was awarded his country's Distinguished Service Medal with the citation:

"For exceptionally meritorious service in a duty of great responsibility before the occupation of French North Africa by the United States Army Forces. As a member of the advance party which effected a successful night landing along the northern coast of the continent and kept a secret rendezvous prior to the outbreak of hostilities, Captain Wright participated in vital military conferences preliminary to the invasion of Morocco and Algeria.

"In addition to assisting in the conception and organisation of plans for offensive operations, he personally commanded the vessel in which General Henri Giraud made his escape from France. His skilful execution of an extremely precarious mission contributed in large measure to the initial success of a highly important objective. . . ."

Jewell's case was made difficult under an arrangement by which British and American officers could receive only one decoration for any special operation—if it resulted in an award by one Government it could not be recognised again by the other. Having received the M.B.E.—on the strength of Barney Fawkes's reports to the Admiralty—the American Government was unable to act upon Clark's recommendation.

In March Jewell was ordered to report to the Flag Officer (Submarines), Rear-Admiral C. B. Barry, D.S.O., at North-ways, his headquarters at Swiss Cottage, London. He was told little there but sent to the Central Intelligence Headquarters in St. James's Street, where he met Squadron Leader Sir Archibald Cholmondeley of Air Intelligence and Lieutenant-Commander Ewen Montagu, R.N.V.R. of Naval Intelligence. From them he learned of "Operation Mincemeat"—a *ruse de guerre* hatched to fool the Germans about Allied plans in the Mediterranean.[1]

They wanted *Seraph* to take an unidentified body of a dead man dressed as a Royal Marine officer to the coast of Spain

---

[1] The full story of this fantastic scheme and its outcome has been told by Ewen Montagu in his book—*The Man Who Never Was* (Evans Brothers).

and drop him close inshore so that he would wash up on the beach. It was hoped that the false papers he was carrying would be found by the Spaniards who would transmit their contents to Germany.

It was a macabre mission which Jewell accepted philosophically on the basis that in wartime any plan which might save lives was worth trying.

Seraph was allowed up from the Blyth Dockyard in April and taken to sea to test her strength after so long in dry dock. She behaved beautifully, riding high when surfaced and steady when submerged. Her new bows, tubes and the extra gun in some respects increased her performance and gave her a lithe, graceful look.

The crew, refreshed and rested, were drilled during a trip round Scotland to Rothesay in the Clyde, where she worked up under realistic war conditions with Atlantic destroyer escorts.

It was usual to have some sort of insignia painted on the conning tower and, by general consent, *Seraph* now sported a picture of Ferdinand the Bull. He had spurned the bullring as had *Seraph* with her special missions outnumbering operational patrols.

On the 18th she tied up alongside the submarine depot ship, H.M.S. *Forth* in Holy Loch, near Rothesay, and a long canister was brought aboard to be stowed in the for'ard torpedo room. The word soon spread round the mess decks that a secret weather reporting buoy was being taken out to the Bay of Biscay for testing. She sailed the next morning for Gibraltar and during the voyage down the Irish Sea, those of the crew whose duties lay in the torpedo room occasionally kicked the canister and joked about "our pal Charlie, the weather man coming for a ride".

Only Jewell knew the truth. Also aboard was something more important to the Eighth Flotilla—a supply of gin, sherry and whisky for distribution in Algiers.

It was an uneventful trip across the Bay and down the coast of Spain, time being spent in continuous diving, surfacing and action drills to recapture that split-second timing so necessary if a submarine was to survive the hazards of the Mediterranean in wartime. Bolton had been transferred and his duties as Gunnery and Torpedo officer were taken over by the stocky meticulous Norris. Edsell had also been relieved and replaced by Lieutenant J. A. Davis.

On the 19th, *Seraph* closed the Spanish coast, dived under a fleet of fishing smacks which crossed her path and before dawn on the 20th was lying three-quarters of a mile off the beach near the mouth of the Huelva river. The crew were ordered below decks while Scott and Sutton heaved the canister through the forehatch to Jewell who was waiting on deck to break the seals. On the bridge, Davis and Norris kept watch for air and surface patrols.

They listened in silence while Jewell explained the reason for the canister, at the same time pulling off the lid and dragging the body carefully on to the deck. Then they took off their caps as he read a short burial service and pushed the body into the sea. The forehatch was closed, *Seraph* turned out to sea and the normal watch took over on the bridge. She had carried out her rôle in "Operation Mincemeat" with no regrets at having been parted from her sightless passenger.

The following morning she entered Gibraltar harbour and Jewell sent a postcard to Montagu in London saying: "Parcel delivered safely."

Seraph returned to Algiers and the battlefield on May 8th and sailed into a bevy of war correspondents and photographers who were hunting for "heroic" stories to mark the victory in Tunisia expected at any day. The crew talked, posed and generally had fun while Jewell was brought up to date by Fawkes aboard *Maidstone*. Meanwhile, the supply of drinks was sent aboard the depot ship for distribution to the Flotilla. That evening the two officers drove to Allied Forces headquarters to be entertained by General Clark.

One of the subjects brought up was the acquisition of a suitable site for a submariners rest camp. Clark told Jewell about some villas on the coast east of Algiers at Sidi Barouck. If he and Fawkes agreed, these could be turned into a camp for officers and men. They thanked Clark and, within a week, Sidi Barouck was officially opened as a camp for weary submariners of the Eighth Flotilla. Clark, ever friendly and wanting to help, generously sent two jeeps with American drivers on permanent loan to act as a bus service between the depot ship and camp. Fawkes invited to dinner Clark and Wright, who was still on the

Supreme Commander's staff, and next day the General left Algiers for his own Fifth Army headquarters at Ouidja in Morocco.

The two sailors involved in the carving knife incident had forgotten their past enmity and were again the best of friends, much to the amusement of their messmates who on occasion still chanted "Three Blind Mice" over drinks ashore.

Seraph, cleansed both physically and morally, sailed from Algiers on the 21st for the Tyrrhenian Sea to carry out an offensive patrol off Sardinia with the object of "sinking enemy warships and supply vessels".

The enemy kept clear of the battlefield until the 27th when, shortly after dusk, two small convoys were sighted steaming close on a parallel course. The nearer consisted of a supply ship escorted by one submarine; the other of three merchant ships led by two armed trawlers. *Seraph* submerged to periscope depth, the attack team closed up in the control room and she moved slowly towards the U-boat. The conning tower was creeping into the sights when a layer of cloud blacked out the moon and the silhouette was lost in the darkness.

Seraph had been on a collision course, so she turned away rapidly and headed for the second convoy. Heavy overcast was forming above and, not to risk losing another target, she surfaced and raced in behind a large trawler to attack the leading merchant ship. Three torpedoes hurtled out in swift succession as she dived; the nearest trawler turned towards her, obviously investigating an echo on her asdics. Jewell took a last glance at the merchantman before falling down the hatch and cursed softly as it altered course to present an end-on target to the torpedoes. Not much hope of a hit there.

She had now to concentrate on dodging depth charges which were close enough to make her shudder slightly, but sufficiently far away to relieve the crew's anxiety. It seemed likely that the enemy had been at sea on anti-submarine exercises when she arrived to give them the opportunity to turn practice into the real thing.

Off Maddalena three days later, they sighted two troop transports escorted by three destroyers. They were at maximum range and going away but Jewell, gazing through the periscope, decided to "fire a torpedo to maintain the offensive only, as it was unlikely the torpedo would reach its target". In taking this decision, he symbolised the feeling of frustration which had fallen over *Seraph* during this patrol. She had been presented with plenty of targets, but for unsatisfactory reasons her attacks had failed. Principal cause was that a submarine needed more than a few practice runs in the Clyde to shake off the lethargy which followed a long home leave.

Prior to ramming the U-boat in December, the crew had been a highly-tuned team with all eyes on the objective of carrying out successful secret missions and destroying the enemy's shipping. Three months in England had been long enough for keyed-up nerves to unwind and become flabby with inaction. The firing of a torpedo at a target it could never hit was an expression of Jewell's irritation at the unsatisfactory state of affairs.

The next morning was like most of the others at that time of the year—calm, smooth, and with little or no wind to ruffle the surface. Not long after 8 a.m. two 3,000-ton supply ships and one destroyer came into the periscope sights. *Seraph* pointed her bows at the leading ship, and Jewell was about to fire when misfortune fell again. As the bow caps of the torpedo tubes opened, air bubbles floated up to burst on the surface in feathery fluffs quickly seen by the destroyer. It turned towards *Seraph* and increased speed, but she held her ground until Jewell had lined up his sights again and fired two torpedoes. He kept the periscope up to watch the tracks and, to his astonishment, the first turned and began circling back towards them.

The periscope came down hurriedly as she dived out of the way listening intently to the torpedo coming round to pass overhead. Even more astonishing, it continued to steer in ever-decreasing circles and crossed above them no less than four times. Suddenly, the submarine trembled in the shock wave of a huge explosion, eyes glanced at stop watches and hopes soared—it was the other torpedo striking home on the target.

Then the depth charges came clattering down, exploding near by with sudden clanging "tonks"—against *Seraph*'s side. She writhed angrily and went deeper with the charges still falling around her but further away. She survived ten patterns of seven charges each before the destroyer returned to help his stricken merchantmen. An hour later, *Seraph* came up to periscope depth. All Jewell could see was a large spreading patch of oil with several pieces of floating wreckage; enough to confirm a hit, but not a kill. It was more likely that the ship had been able to limp to safety under the watchful eye of the destroyer.

For the next ten days *Seraph* saw little in the Maddalena area other than the continuous comings and goings of aircraft. A month ago these would almost certainly have been German or Italian; now they were British or American—one of the changes brought about by the victory in Tunisia.

Once an enemy destroyer was seen racing across the horizon obviously too intent on private thoughts to worry much about the possibility of being watched through a periscope. But this was the only sign of surface life and, at dawn on June 10th, *Seraph* snuggled wearily aginst *Maidstone*'s ample side and settled down to rest, frustrated at the lack of targets and disgusted at her performance with those which had provided any reasonable hope of success.

Captain Fawkes was none too pleased when he read the account of the torpedo fired to "maintain the offensive" but tempered his criticism by reminding Jewell that it had been more of a working up patrol than an operational one. "Your chaps had to shake down into the routine again. After this they'll do better next time."

The first night in harbour was spent aboard *Maidstone* but next day one of Clark's jeeps took the crew to the new rest camp at Sidi Barouck. Their driver was Private Bocciccio, an effervescent caustic wit from Brooklyn, who rode his jeep sidesaddle with one leg permanently placed on the driver's wing outside.

Sidi Barouck proved an exclusive spot with several rows of guards, all of whom wanted plenty of evidence of identity before the crew were allowed to pass. Private Bocciccio had an undying admiration for the submariners of *Maidstone* and he fixed the last guard with a mean look: "Look, guy, these boys is tired an' they want in. What the hell you fellas got in there, anyway? The Queen of Sheba in the Nood?"

The North African war had lasted six months from the time

of the Allied landings to the day Von Arnim surrendered in Tunisia—a period during which the submarines of the Eighth Flotilla had played more than an ordinary share in the enemy's defeat. Sir Andrew Cunningham's Report on the naval war showed that the Mediterranean submarines had sunk 1,335,000 tons of enemy shipping of which 760,000 tons had been destined for North Africa only. According to the statistical experts, this figure represented a loss to the enemy of 48,000 men; 126,000 tons of oil; 1,300 tanks; 4,000 heavy guns; 260 howitzers; 700 armoured cars; 1,550 Bren carriers; 156,000 tons of ammunition; 18,000 rifles; 74,000 tons of tank and general equipment; and 188 ships themselves. These estimates were worked out from a normal war load carried by a merchant ship with 30 per cent. deducted to allow for unknown factors and exaggeration.

This feat of arms had not been cheaply won. Forty-one British submarines had been lost—six from Fawkes's own flotilla.

In the same period the R.A.F. had made 542 strikes against ships at sea and 1,367 sorties against harbours. In these attacks three ships were sunk and twenty-one damaged. This was not, perhaps, as fair a comparison as it should have been, for the R.A.F. were using ancient planes entirely unsuitable for attacking ships at sea.

This report stressed the bitter controversy raging behind the scenes between the Navy and the R.A.F. on the subject of sea policy.

"The R.A.F. at this time were hampered by unsuitable aircraft and lack of practice against ships as is shown by their efficiency which was only 33 per cent. against that of 68 per cent. by the Fleet Air Arm operating old Swordfish and Albacores, but nevertheless highly trained.

"The high price our submarines have paid for their success will be justified if the R.A.F. and U.S.A.A.F. are convinced of the important part sea power plays in overseas campaigns and of the necessity of sinking ships; and will then attack ships on a greater scale—a scale expected of a Great Maritime Power."

Captain Fawkes had contributed to this overall picture with his own analysis of the Eighth Flotilla's impact on the western Mediterranean. "In the six months since TORCH was launched," he said, "submarines of the Eighth Flotilla have sunk or damaged more than a quarter of a million tons of enemy shipping. Three thousand torpedoes have been fired of which 30 per cent. have hit. A further 10,000 tons have been sunk by gun actions.

"We mourn, however, the loss of *Turbulent*, *Tigris*, *Thunderbolt*, *Sahib*, *P-222* and *Splendid*. With the exception of *Turbulent*'s loss by mine, the remaining five were all lost as a result of depth charge attacks—a hazard which every submarine commanding officer knows he has to face."

These were *Seraph*'s sisters, fledgling youngsters who had grown up too quickly, only to be killed too soon. In them had been friends, and their ghosts hovered close whenever *Seraph* rocked under the blast of depth charges. This dread weapon was tucked carefully away into the subconscious to become a permanent feature of their lives.

Yet tremendous satisfaction flowed through the Flotilla when Captain Fawkes distributed copies of the Commander-in-Chief's reply to his Report. Sir Andrew's letter read:

"It is appropriate that your Report covers the period from the initial landings in North Africa to the expulsion of the Axis from the continent. To the great victory which has been achieved, and of which we are reaping the fruits today, the submarines of the Eighth Flotilla have contributed a vitally important share; how important is perhaps only realised by those whose profession is the sea. I am sure that the greatest source of satisfaction to you, the commanding officers and ships companies of the Flotilla, is the knowledge that the Navy itself realises the full extent of the contribution that had been made to the battle by the submarines. Your achievement has been great, but the price has not been light. Yet the standard of the Submarine Service, a standard it sets itself, has been maintained throughout."

During this rest ashore two unusual events took place in the life of Bill Jewell. Rosemary Galloway, a Wren officer he had once met in England, arrived in Algiers to join the Allied Forces Headquarters cypher staff and became his constant companion in off-duty hours; the second was an invitation

that all his crew should visit General Mark Clark's headquarters at Ouidja in French Morocco where he was training
the Fifth Army for the long battle ahead in Italy. Captain
Fawkes had also been invited and two Dakota aircraft,
Clark's personal planes, arrived at Algiers to pick up the
submariners.

Jewell had to leave a watch aboard *Seraph*, so with Fawkes
and himself there were two more officers and nearly twenty
assorted petty officers and ratings. They climbed into the
aircraft and for the next hour flew over the sandy, mountainous
hinterland of French North Africa. At noon the planes lost
height and soon landed on an airstrip near the headquarters.

To the astonishment of the crew, Clark had organised his
Army as though it were being visited by Eisenhower himself.
A company had been turned out in battledress and white-
painted helmets to form a 50-yard guard of honour which
Clark insisted that the sailors inspect with their officers. The
next stop was a long, low building in which they sat at a row of
tables for lunch. Afterwards, there were cars to take them to
nearby towns and villages on sightseeing tours. "Nothing's
too good for the boys who made this the most bloodless invasion imaginable," Clark kept repeating.

They slept at Headquarters that night and, after breakfast,
Clark shook hands with everyone again before they boarded
the two planes for the return to Algiers. He took Jewell to one
side and whispered: "You know, Bill, I'm sore about you not
getting something from us for those trips before the landings.
I've had a word with Ike and he thinks we can get round this
agreement between our Governments by making an award to
Seraph. Ike's having his staff check the details and, if it can be
done, he will make an announcement."

He looked at Fawkes. "That's about the best we can do,
Barney. Did you hear, they gave me the Legion of Merit—
that's Ike's doing."

Jewell felt better after that talk. It would be another unique
stroke of fortune if *Seraph* received a decoration—she would be
the only one among all their sisters in the Submarine Service to
have a medal rivetted to her conning tower. He would still
keep Ferdinand, of course.

Once back in Algiers, Captain Fawkes was not long in

preparing sailing orders for *Seraph*—her crew had done enough junketing and could now be expected to work for it. And as compensation for the disappointments of the previous patrol, he assigned her to the work she liked best—another secret mission.

CHAPTER ELEVEN

"HUSKY"

ON June 22nd, Jewell received orders to take secret equipment aboard, exercise it outside Algiers until the next morning and proceed to Oran where *Seraph*'s presence was urgently required by Lieutenant-General George Patton, commander of the United States Seventh Army, and Admiral A. G. Kirk, U.S. Navy, commander of the Western Task Force.

"You are," said Fawkes casually, "to act as guide and beacon submarine for the Army's invasion of Sicily."

The equipment sent aboard was a new type of buoy which acted as a "homing" beacon to lost ships. With this method, destroyers leading flotillas of landing craft into beaches during darkness could "home" on the buoy, thereby ensuring that her troop-filled charges hit the right beach and not someone else's.

Next day, they practised laying the buoy until the crew could "arm" and lay it in the dark almost silently—when the time came they would be doing it only yards from the enemy beach at night. In the evening *Seraph* made the passage to Oran on the surface.

On arrival, she tied up alongside the battleship H.M.S. *Howe*, and Jewell reported aboard the U.S.S. *Biscayne*, Admiral Kirk's flagship. The Admiral was friendly, invited him to stay for dinner and told him what was expected of *Seraph*. Patton's army was to land on the southern shore of Sicily near Gela at midnight on the 9th, but intelligence of what they might expect to meet was sadly lacking and beach reconnaissance not very satisfactory. The submarine was to arrive off Sicily on the 6th, dive close inshore and observe the beaches, reporting any movements ashore and checking the contours and gradients of the coastline against the intelligence reports, copies of which would be supplied. After dark on the 9th she was to drop her "homing" buoy off the beach and remain stationary on the surface to act as guiding beacon for the first waves of the invasion force.

Next day, Jewell was taken inland to 7th Army Headquarters to meet Patton himself. Whatever that fiery, two-gun General thought of some British military leaders he had a healthy respect for the Royal Navy and made no secret of it. In a few quick words to Admiral Kirk and Jewell he explained his requirements. His force was to land in three parts, each on its own beach; he wanted reconnaissance checked and the submarines allocated to the beaches to stay in their position over the beacon buoys to ensure that the right forces landed on the right beaches. The submarines would be less than a mile from the enemy, but come what may they must stay there until the Task Force with the Army arrived, no matter how late. Jewell wondered who the other submarines were and Kirk brought the information that two sisters of the Eighth Flotilla—*Safari* and *Shakespeare*, then at Bizerta and Algiers respectively—would also act as beacons.

Code names for the three landing groups were—Yellow Force to be guided to Blue Beach by *Seraph* (code name "Cent"); Green Force to Green Beach guided by *Safari* (code name "Dime"); and Red Force to Red Beach by *Shakespeare* (code name "Joss").

After the conference, Jewell heard a loud voice call his name. It was an old friend from the Galita reconnaissance mission, Colonel Bill Darby of the U.S. Rangers. After exchanging greetings, they discussed the invasion and Jewell found that the Rangers were to be part of the force landing on his beach.

"Do as good a job for us as you did at Galita, Bill, and we'll be mighty grateful," said the Colonel who left suddenly in answer to a summons from another high-ranking American officer, Major-General Terry Allen, legendary leader of the Ranger battalion. Yellow Force was to be led in the assault by Patton's second in command, a general whose name was just becoming known in world headlines—Omar Bradley.

After leaving the headquarters, Jewell returned to *Seraph* with orders to carry out further exercises off Oran before sailing on the 4th for Sicily.

They made an uneventful passage across the 100-odd miles to Sicily and approached the beaches on either side of Gela and Licata at dawn on the 6th. Through the periscope the

officers studied the coastline, checked it against earlier reconnaissance reports and made any necessary alterations by radio
to Patton's headquarters. On the 7th, *Safari* and *Shakespeare*
arrived and the three submarines took up patrols a mile or so
off their respective beaches.

At night they withdrew into the outfield to surface and
charge batteries while bombers of the R.A.F. and U.S.A.A.F.
swept overhead on saturation raids to soften up the island on
which 300,000 German and Italian troops were known to be
stationed. These raids had been carried out nightly for nearly a
month and it did not need a genius to recognise them as the
prelude to an invasion. Jewell wondered idly if "Charlie",
the dead man he had formally buried at sea off the Spanish coast
six weeks before, had delivered his false information to the
Germans and whether, as a result, the thousands of troops
already preparing to assault the island would meet less resistance
than they might normally have expected.

If the enemy had kept 300,000 men in Sicily it seemed hardly
likely that he could have transferred much of his strength to
Sardinia or Corsica.

During the 8th, *Seraph* moved in to within a few hundred
yards of a small, sandy area marked on the charts as Blue Beach.
The periscope poked up and, through it, the positions of
navigation buoys, lighthouses, evidence of gun emplacements
and roadways leading from the beach were plotted and coded
into signals for Admiral Kirk.

At dusk she withdrew again, surfaced when the shadows of
night had fallen, and charged batteries—a full store of power
would be needed. At midnight, she closed the beach again
and the crew brought out on deck small marker buoys with
time-fused blinker lights. As *Seraph* steamed down either side
of the approach the small buoys were dropped overboard.
Before dawn, she retired seawards and submerged for the day
vigil.

The 7th Army had embarked and the Western Task Force
was already at sea. OPERATION HUSKY had begun.

At 10 p.m. on the 9th, *Seraph* surfaced and crept in towards
the beach again, this time to stop about a mile out for the most
difficult task of dropping the beacon buoy. She was in position
and the buoy was being brought up for rigging on deck when a

look-out suddenly announced softly: "E-boat on port quarter, sir."

In the still night air his report had the impact of a shout and, when Jewell and his officers on the bridge turned, there was no need for binoculars. The rakish enemy boat was a clearly visible silhouette standing out blackly against the dark blueness of the night. The sea was choppy and a nudging swell made *Seraph* roll sharply; the enemy was proceeding slowly, obviously carrying out an anti-invasion patrol in the hope of sighting the fleets of landing craft in time to signal a warning.

All movement on deck and below ceased as the crew waited tensely for the E-boat to make his move. It was inconceivable that *Seraph* had not been seen. The cruel agony of suspense mounted as both ships—the submarine much lower in the water and presenting an infinitely smaller silhouette—seemed to gaze at each other estimating their chances. At a whispered order, *Seraph*'s gun-crews tip-toed to action stations, the torpedo men manned the torpedo room and the attack team closed up in the control room. The enemy had three times *Seraph*'s speed and their equivalent in fire power, but Jewell might have to silence him. Discovery at that moment would throw the whole HUSKY plan into jeopardy.

Suddenly, the E-boat flashed on his navigation lights: he had sighted *Seraph* and was undecided about her identity expecting only friendly submarines so near his coast. This moment of indecision in which he preferred to challenge rather than attack gave *Seraph* her opportunity to escape. Decks were cleared, the buoy manhandled below again, the "lid" slammed tight, and down she went in a few seconds to scrape the bottom as she headed seawards. The whole operation was carried out with the sort of speed only attained by an efficient, well-trained crew; to the enemy, she must have seemed literally to vanish. The captain of the E-boat would still be victim to his own indecision for even a friendly submarine would quite naturally dive out of sight at the appearance of a surface vessel she could not identify.

Jewell was delighted with his men; at last they had shaken off the hangover of long home leave, and their behaviour in the past few minutes had been that of veterans.

Twenty minutes later, the enemy's propeller noises faded

and *Seraph* came up for a look around. Only an hour was left to midnight, the invasion deadline. Surfaced, she moved in again, the beacon buoy back on deck and rigged for dropping overboard. The gun crews were at action stations, ready to end the perplexity of any inquisitive E-boat suddenly. There could be no more diving—this time the buoy had to be laid.

Mercifully, there was no further interference from the enemy. Instead, it came from ashore just before midnight when coastal radar picked up the approach of the Task Force. *Seraph* was wallowing jerkily above the buoy which was already "homing" the destroyer escorting the landing craft from the troopships to the "release point". All was more than usually quiet when the faint throb of approaching engines drifted across the water—Yellow Force coming in. Then it was daylight. The deep midnight blue was suddenly jerked aside by a curtain of light from a battery of searchlights ashore. Their blindingly brilliant beams cut across the water and blended into a dazzling ball of light concentrated on *Seraph*. She had just recovered from the shock when the first red flashes and loud cracks of the shore batteries gave only split second warning of shells whining overhead. Another gun emplacement joined in while the searchlights fixed her in a tight glaring grip. This was no place for *Seraph*. One hit in her ballast tanks or penetration of her hull and she was useless as a submarine. In normal circumstances she would now have retired gracefully underwater.

But these were not normal circumstances; Yellow Force was coming in and, above the roar of gunfire, *Seraph* could hear the sound of approaching ships growing louder. It was at once essential for her to hold her position until the first wave of troops had passed and could be guided on the last lap by the marker buoys. That was military logic—more final, it was Patton's order.

The shells were falling around her now, some salvoes just over, the next short and the rest straddling her. The crew grimly recognised that they had to stay and the cook at the 3-inch gun could be heard muttering threats and curses rarely heard in his galley. Spray from falling shot drenched the bridge and the watch on deck huddled behind the sides of the conning tower as much to avoid the cascading water as to find protection from flying shrapnel.

Ten more minutes—a nerve-tightening, shell-packed eternity to *Seraph*—before Admiral Kirk in the U.S.S. *Biscayne* saw her plight and a cruiser squadron formed into line ahead three miles out, steamed opposite the beach and fired a series of broadsides at the shore defences. Now *Seraph* was really in the middle, in a watery no-man's-land with lines of red dots marking the guns on both sides. Shells whistled high overhead, but one shore battery maintained a deadly-looking concentration on *Seraph*, still fixed in the bull's-eye of the searchlights.

The sound of approaching ships became a steady throbbing beat as their dark shapes emerged slowly from the shadows cast by a cloud-swept sky, a destroyer leading in long columns of landing craft.

The marker buoys blinked on and the destroyer's guns joined the chorus of gunfire, aiming at the searchlights which now blinded her and the force behind. She rounded *Seraph*, her crew cheering the stubborn little submarine; then the landing craft chugged to run ashore between the marker buoys. *Seraph* sighed with relief; her job was done and Yellow Force had hit Blue Beach accurately. Now she could slide wearily back into the protective darkness.

First, however, she wanted to take her seat in the stalls and watch the curtain go up ashore. The enemy lights went out and now it was our own searchlights playing on the shore like footlights on a stage. Tiny darting flashes marked the progress of the assault force as their tommy-guns blazed a path through the defenders. Jewell thought grimly that one of those guns might be Bill Darby's for it was like him to be first ashore. He hoped the friendly, ever-joking colonel would do nothing foolhardy.

A look-out's voice announced the approach of a landing craft with a four-ringed captain standing in the stern. It was Admiral Kirk's chief of staff.

"Ahoy *Seraph*," he called out. "The Admiral has sent me over to thank you personally in his name for a great job of work."

The crew were momentarily stunned. What sort of Navy was it that sent full captains barging about in the middle of a battle to say nice things to small ships commanded by very junior officers? Jewell gave a slightly astonished salute and shouted back: "Thank you, sir."

"Yeah, I want to thank you myself, too," called back the captain, insisting that this assault involving hundreds of thousands of men was just the place for an exchange of polite pleasantries. "You know, those boys who landed are going to remember for a long time how you guided 'em in. You could 've gotten to hell out of that trap and left 'em on their own. The Admiral thinks you did just fine, boys, and so do we all. Good luck, I gotta get back."

The landing craft's engines burst into life taking him into the darkness where the flagship made a huge black blob in the night. *Seraph* shook herself back to reality. Surely Admirals like this in Navies like this existed only in the dreams of junior officers who at best could look forward to a curt "well done".

Reflecting on the strange yet extremely acceptable ways of her ally, *Seraph* returned to the firework show. Enemy aircraft had joined the battle dropping flares over the invasion fleets which, when illuminated, became the targets of their gunners and bombers.

Off the next beach lay *Safari*, having guided Green Force in to land and now also waiting around to enjoy the show. Suddenly a brief whistle rent the air and a stick of bombs fell across her, two near misses lifting her bodily out of the water and dumping her back again with a loud crash. She suffered only several bloody noses and bruised bodies, but behind her the destroyer, U.S.S. *Maddox*, which had led in the first wave of Green Force to the release point marked by *Safari* caught a 500-lb. bomb on her quarter deck. She sank in three minutes, with all hands lost. Frantic searches for survivors in which *Safari* joined proved fruitless. The destroyer had been blown to pieces and her crew with her.

Safari withdrew out of danger. At Red Beach, conditions had been easier. *Shakespeare* was able to bring her assault forces in unmolested and retire to watch the excitement.

An American PT boat—similar to the British motor-torpedo boat—came alongside *Seraph* and flashed. "I've been sent to take you out of here and put you on the way to Malta. If you're all set we'll get going."

Seraph replied that she was ready and her engines throbbed to full speed as she followed in the wake of the PT boat.

It was a quiet trip back until an hour before dawn on the 10th, *Seraph* was about 300 yards astern of the PT boat when a stentorian shout was heard from the sea on the starboard side.

"Help, Help."

Those lungs were in excellent condition. The PT boat heard the cry stopped while the lonely swimmer paddled alongside where willing hands pulled him aboard. He was an American soldier who had been part of the assault force for Red Beach. En route in a transport, he had tumbled overboard and lost his way. Once he realised he could not possibly arrive in Sicily with his buddies and, concerned lest he drown like a sailor might instead of being mown down by enemy machine-gun fire, like a good infantryman should, he had wisely divested himself of all battle accoutrements and other obstacles to the business of staying afloat.

During the morning, Jewell decided to exercise the machine-guns. He talked to the PT boat and suggested they join in a little target practice. The American captain declined with thanks. Although he would have liked to pit his crew's firing skill against *Seraph*, he regretted they had no ammunition aboard. Before leaving Oran the lockers had been cleared and all available space filled with cases of Coca-Cola for the flotilla to which he belonged.

It seemed that the silence which greeted this explanation called for further clarification. "You see," he continued, "once we heard we were going to Sicily we knew we would be based there and naturally there would be no Coca-Cola supplies. We drew lots and my boat was elected to become the supply ship for the flotilla. I couldn't tell the Admiral that when he detailed me to escort you."

Last night an admiral had sent his chief of staff to thank them in the fierce heat of a raging battle; now a junior officer of the same Navy admitted he had taken his ship on an assault of enemy territory armed with cases of Coca-Cola!

"Anyway, I think we've come far enough with you boys," went on the American brightly. "Think you can look after yourselves now?"

Jewell leant weakly against the conning tower, not quite sure if he should laugh or cry.

With a cheerful wave, the PT boat captain gave orders to his helmsman and with a great, powerful roar the engines started up and she headed back towards Sicily, a sleek, dangerous looking warship with only *Seraph* to know that her menace was phoney, the curving threat of her bow wave empty of bite.

They arrived at Malta that afternoon to find *Safari* and *Shakespeare* already there. Malta was a very relieved fortress by then with repair work already in hand and food beginning to become adequate after so many long months of siege by the Luftwaffe. Eisenhower and Admiral Cunningham had set up temporary headquarters on the island and the three submarine commanding officers were invited to dine with them that evening.

The Supreme Commander and Naval Commander-in-Chief had already heard of the successful landings made possible by the three sisters of the Eighth Flotilla and the dinner was their way of saying "thank you" to the slightly overawed young officers—at least two were overawed, *Seraph*'s commander being more accustomed to intimate contact with Admirals and Generals. After all, he had a full captain as spiritual co-commander.

Two days later, *Seraph* was escorted into Algiers flying her Jolly Roger, with the strange devices indicating enemy ships sunk and special missions successfully completed, alongside the White Ensign. Once tied up to *Maidstone* there was a rush for baths, shaves and clean clothes.

The spell in harbour was cut short by the success of the Sicily landings. The Germans were building up a formidable opposition in Italy, Sardinia and Corsica; submarines were needed in the Tyrrhenian Sea to intercept their transports and supply ships on the island run. A brief two days at the rest camp, two days in Algiers itself and the crew were back on board preparing *Seraph* for another voyage. Jewell tried to find out if "Charlie" had really affected the outcome in Sicily; but this was impossible to estimate, he was told. The number of German and Italian troops on Sicily had exceeded 300,000 and Patton's Seventh Army had made rapid progress inland only because the enemy had expected the invasion to be launched on the western coast instead of the southern. He had massed in the west and left other coasts only lightly defended. By the time he realised his mistake, he was faced by the British, Canadian and American Armies all solidly entrenched inland. There was nothing for it but to fight stubbornly and build another line of defence in Italy and the Tyrrhenian islands.

Before sailing there were more changes among *Seraph*'s officers. Sutton, the sharp-witted, slight, sandy-haired Warrant Engineer, was transferred, to the dismay of everyone from Jewell down. He had been not only an efficient and hard-working engineer, but a jack-of-all-trades able to make almost anything with his capable hands. Fortunately, his successor, Mr. M. N. Stevenson, filled his shoes more than adequately. An extra officer arrived called Harris, a short, square-faced dark Lieutenant R.N.V.R. who had left a thriving North Country business to become a wartime sailor. The Wardroom was now overcrowded by the addition of one, and the original officers prayed there would be no more trips involving passengers. Meanwhile, they put out with orders to sink on sight any vessel met in the Tyrrhenian Sea.

Recently it had become standard procedure for submarines to be escorted for their first day out on the surface. On arrival they would be met by an escort and approach harbour on the surface. This procedure was in force on July 15th when *Seraph* sailed on her eighth Mediterranean patrol.

A strong breeze was blowing from the starboard beam as she headed north, choppy, rising seas causing her to cannon from one high wave to another. She had no liking for this and strained to wriggle from the troughs in which her design made her travel. Above, the blue sky was streaked with foamy cloud which threatened to amass until finally the sun was blotted out by a thick layer of overcast.

It was very dark and, shortly before midnight, she was trying desperately to keep station on her hurrying escort when a convoy of landing craft was seen crossing her bows from port to starboard. What might have been a PT or an E-boat came too close to *Seraph* who at once flashed recognition signals. The dark shape blinked a reply which made no sense at all. *Seraph* was beginning to become worried when her signalman reported that the mysterious signals from the approaching ship were the recognition signals for the previous day and, therefore, thoroughly out-of-date and suspect.

Jewell was considering drastic action when at last the stranger identified himself as an American PT boat acting as escort to the landing craft. They tried to persuade him to look up the correct challenge and reply for the present period, but the American insisted he was right and *Seraph* wrong. Jewell would have liked to call up his own escort to prove the point, but as he wrote later in his Report: "Our escort was so far ahead as to be useless."

The correct recognition was at last established and the PT ran off to catch up with his now unescorted charges.

An hour later, *Seraph*'s escort took her leave, rapidly exchanging only the barest courtesies and rushed off back to Algiers and whatever had been interrupted by a thoughtless submarine.

At dawn, Jewell took *Seraph* down to periscope depth for two reasons—firstly, because it was the custom to dive at dawn and, secondly, because a craft had appeared in the pale glow to the east. This proved to be the Italian hospital ship, *Virgilio*, and *Seraph* was content to make two dummy attacks on her before she passed on unaware of the fate that might have been hers had she been sailing under anything but the Red Cross banner.

There followed the most disappointing, monotonous patrol of her career. She scoured the Tyrrhenian for targets and found nothing; she lurked pugnaciously off the harbour mouths and rocky promontories of Corsica and Sardinia only to draw a blank. It seemed that the enemy was hugging the mainland.

On the 25th, *Seraph* was ordered to undertake a special patrol off Corsica. Intelligence had warned Captain Fawkes that partisan leaders demanded to be picked up and brought to Algiers for conferences with General Giraud who was in command of a French army already ear-marked to occupy the Tyrrhenian islands. But before giving the Allies the assistance they needed, the partisans wanted a formal undertaking that the French would not remain in permanent occupation. Giraud, as representative of an imperialist nation, was not trusted by the islanders.

Deadline for the pick-up was midnight, but by 3 a.m. *Seraph* was still patrolling along the rendezvous waiting for the shoreboat to appear. By dawn there was no sign of the boat or of activity ashore and reluctantly she dived away from the island. Two hours of uncertainty about the next move was ended by a signal from Fawkes ordering her back to her original patrol area. Once again she had been cheated of the excitement needed to relieve the boredom of sailing an empty sea.

By the 27th they were resigned to scoring nil and there were loud ironic cheers when they turned southwards to head for home. They sailed into Algiers at dawn on the 27th wearing only the White Ensign—a blank patrol did not justify the flying of the Jolly Roger. When Fawkes came aboard as usual and heard of their "duck", he merely chuckled.

"That's nothing to worry about," he told Jewell. "The enemy knew you were there all right and your presence forced them to disrupt their normal traffic between Italy and the islands. It was not exactly a morale-boosting patrol but it served its purpose. Anyway, get your chaps down to the rest camp for a bit and then we'll see. I think there's something interesting coming up. Just the sort of job *Seraph* likes. I'll keep you posted."

With that enigmatic remark, he left a disgruntled Jewell thinking that whatever was in store had to be pretty exciting to wash away the taste of the last two weeks. He looked sourly at the innocently smiling and placid Ferdinand on his conning tower.

CHAPTER TWELVE

IKE'S CADILLAC

C APTAIN FAWKES glanced again at the message on his desk. It was a signal, signed "Jellicoe", from Combined Operations Headquarters asking that Captain A. R. McClair of the Special Boat Section be granted an interview and given help within reason.

Since the landings in North Africa, Fawkes had been plagued by Combined Operations with its offshoots called the Special Boat Section; Inshore Special Service Unit, Special Operations Executive and Special Air Service; then had come the O.S.S.—Office of Strategic Services, an American organisation; more recently he had met the Deuxième Bureau, a North African version of the famed pre-war French secret service. They all wanted him to provide submarines for their nefarious activities. Curiously, one organisation never told the other what it was doing.

He reflected bitterly on a recent case in which the O.S.S. had wanted a submarine to take a party to Rome where they had business with the Vatican. The S.O.E. had wanted a submarine at the same time to take a party to Rome where they wished to blow up a bridge. Both parties refused to travel in the same submarine! Fawkes had appealed to the Commander-in-Chief who had been advised by an army liaison officer to release the submarines.

The result: the S.O.E. had landed first, blown up the bridge and retired; two days later the O.S.S. had landed at the same spot, reached the sabotaged bridge and as the detour would delay them twenty-four hours and upset their schedule they had abandoned their mission and returned to the submarine. Meanwhile, one of the submarines had been badly depth charged and would be out of commission for at least four months. No wonder Fawkes looked at this latest request with angry suspicion.

Captain McClair was shown into his office, a young carefree

officer with just the faintest hint of the swashbuckler about him. Fawkes groaned inwardly.

"Well, what is it you want?"

"A submarine, please sir," replied the young man confidently.

Fawkes blanched. "Would you care to give me the reason?"

"Well, sir, I'm not sure that I should. Job's frightfully hush-hush, you know."

Fawkes hoped he looked suitably impressed. "Really, now. You know I meet a lot of you fellows from time to time and I always insist on knowing the reason before I hand over a submarine. They're rather expensive toys to be chucked around casually."

"Well, I've been told to take a party to Italy, sir. You see, we are in contact with the partisan forces behind the German lines there and they want certain equipment. They have tremendous military value, these chaps, with masses of guerilla activities which cause Jerry no end of trouble, you know. Now they must have some radios, machine-guns, pistols and ammunition, sir. So we want to dump it somewhere along a convenient bit of coast and tell them where to pick it up."

"I see," replied Fawkes wearily. "Are you sure you can't get it to them any other way?"

"No, sir. Air would bungle the thing somehow—you know how they work, don't you, sir." The young officer said this with the air of a superior conspirator.

"Oh, yes, of course, you're so right," said Fawkes not really knowing why the Air Force should not drop this sort of stuff. He seemed to have heard that they were doing it pretty well in France and the Low Countries.

"In any event, they've said they can't spare the aircraft, sir," went on McClair. Fawkes sat back. This was the real reason, he thought. So, as a last resort, Jellicoe was trying for a submarine.

"All right, McClair, I'll place the matter before the Commander-in-Chief. If he says you can have a submarine then you may look over the side of this ship and take your pick."

Captain McClair rose to his feet, saluted and left the room. Fawkes drafted a signal to Sir Andrew Cunningham suitably worded to give the impression that there were no submarines available.

About the same time as McClair left *Maidstone*, Bill Jewell was escorting a party of Wren officers on an inspection of *Seraph*. Among them was Rosemary Galloway and it seemed to his officers that she was getting most of their captain's attention. The C-in-C's orders allowed women aboard His Majesty's ships only at the commanding officer's discretion and, in the case of submarines, that meant Captain Fawkes. In this instance, discretion had been suitably applied and the girls had reached the end of their tour—the Wardroom.

They were among the last women to visit a warship at Algiers. That night Fawkes gave a small party for Mark Clark and General Eisenhower. To give colour to the proceedings he had also invited two American Red Cross girls, both fun-loving in off-duty hours, a Wren officer, Jewell, Rosemary Galloway and Kay Summersby, Eisenhower's attractive driver.

The Supreme Commander could stay only for drinks as he was dining that night with "ABC". Kay drove back to his villa and returned to *Maidstone* with the car, a new Cadillac, only recently arrived for the exclusive use of Eisenhower. The car was parked on the jetty, nearly opposite *Maidstone*'s mole.

The party was getting into its stride when the air raid warning screeched. It announced not the approach of enemy aircraft but the discovery of Italian saboteurs in the harbour. Action stations sounded and the party broke up, the girls being told to grab their coats and prepare to leave. Kay was worried about the Cadillac, wanted to drive it to shelter but agreed to take the rest of the women with her. They had just reached the bottom of the gangway when there was a tremendous explosion on the jetty opposite *Maidstone*. An erratic torpedo loosed off by a sabotage team had circled round *Maidstone*, hit the jetty and blown up the Cadillac.

Within a few minutes the enemy were caught, and the party re-assembled in Fawkes's cabin. Kay Summersby telephoned the Supreme Commander to break the news about his Cadillac. Eisenhower explained that it was not her fault and told her to enjoy herself. He would walk to Admiral Cunningham's headquarters for dinner.

Next morning, the the fate of Eisenhower's car was known throughout Algiers. Captain Fawkes reported to the Commander-in-Chief's headquarters to discuss the request of

Combined Operations for a submarine. "ABC" thought it was reasonable and told Fawkes to place one at McClair's disposal.

Aboard *Maidstone*, Fawkes paced the quarter deck for a while and then reached a decision. *Seraph* had returned with bad luck from her last patrol. She would take McClair and his party to Italy. This was the sort of thing she did better than most, and at least she could be relied upon to bring the Army back safely.

Two days after this affair, Jewell called for Rosemary at the Wrennery to take her to the Hotel St. George where they were to dine with Jerry Wright. He was driving an ancient Hillman of obscure origin which the Eighth Flotilla had acquired, and known throughout Algiers as "The Wren Trap". The name was well-deserved, for none of the doors opened from the inside and, no matter how urgent the need for fresh air, Wrens who accepted the risk had to rely on the chivalry of their companions to release them.

When Private Bocciccio saw an officer drive away from *Maidstone* in the Hillman instead of using his jeep, he would show his teeth and snort derisively: "Bloody"—an expressive word he had picked up through long association with *Maidstone*— "heap ain't got no bloody springs left."

Meanwhile, at least three of the crew were adequately supplied with such luxuries as tinned fruit and Coca-Cola. A large American supply dump had been set up near the submarine jetty. They now organised a system by which one would call the American sentry over to *Seraph* to gossip while the other two made a quick sortie into the dump emerging with the most convenient crate. It was always a moment of surprise to open it and find out what had been scrounged. Invariably it turned out to be Coca-Cola or tinned fruit.

Another reliable source of supply was the American nurses, good friends of *Seraph*. All submarines carried a ration of sweets for the crews to chew when submerged. This was particularly helpful to smokers who could ward off the craving for a cigarette. Once they heard this, the American girls rushed to the Army stores and bought pounds of gums, boiled sweets and chocolates which were showered upon *Seraph*.

To the sailors who preferred wandering round Algiers to the

"rest camp", there was much on offer. The town rose from the shore up a steep hill to where the old Moorish town built round the ancient fortress of the Beys looked down upon the new city built by the French on the harbour itself. The two were connected by a steep, narrow, jagged street called the Kasbah. They could seek entertainment of a more orthodox kind in the European community of the new city or Arabian adventure by climbing the Kasbah to the old Moorish town with its windowless houses and hundreds of peepholes covered with iron gratings. Yet despite their hungry hunt for pleasure which would drown the memories of minefields and depth charge attacks, they were less colourful inheritors of a port made notorious by the Barbary pirates 300 years before.

In these surroundings the long days in the cramped, instrument-filled quarters of *Seraph* were forgotten. Anxiety, fears, domestic worries and personal squabbles could always be ironed out under the sun in a French café or a Moorish bar.

Jewell was proud of his ship and those who manned her. They were veterans of eight patrols into enemy waters and *Seraph* was as efficient as any submarine in the Service. More Allied victories and continuous enemy withdrawals both at sea and on land brought a feeling of confidence which no artificially inspired morale-boosting could equal. None of the crew had requested a transfer and there were no trouble-makers to be transferred.

Seraph herself was again showing signs of wear; only internally were the signs of care visible. Brass shone, metal valve handles gleamed, the diesel pistons sparkled from hours of patient polishing and thin layers of clean engine oil over all the bright work gave evidence of regular attention. Throughout the passage-way through the bulkheads which separated the compartments there was an air of orderliness with movables stowed neatly into place so that nothing was in the way. Living in *Seraph* was a tight affair, but it was as clean, tidy and spacious as a meticulous First Lieutenant, David Scott, could make it.

His fastidiousness was not without reason: *Seraph* had passed from childhood quickly, and now was growing older more rapidly than was normal under the conditions of war. She had begun to feel the need of affectionate hands to massage life into her tiring mechanism and over-worked engines—the latter could wish for none more clever than those of her new engineer, Stevenson. For it was on her efficient working that the safety of her crew depended. Whether on secret mission or operational patrol their only link with Algiers and home was *Seraph*. Faulty mechanism, tired engines or sluggish steering gear could mean disaster. If only for that reason there were no drones aboard her.

This knowledge gave Jewell a quiet confidence when he was called into Fawkes's office on August 26th to be introduced to McClair and briefed on his coming voyage.

"Now, Bill," said the Captain, "you are going back to the Tyrrhenian, but don't think it's going to be another patrol like the last one. Remember I told you I might have something more up *Seraph*'s street when you came back last time? Well, this is it. McClair and his party want to take some secret equipment to the Italian mainland.

"They would like to be taken inshore a little to the right of Genoa where they will select a likely place for paddling the stuff ashore, burying it and coming back with you. Actually I've compromised a bit with McClair. When the operation is completed, you will patrol between Corsica and the mainland. I think that might prove more profitable than down the Sardinia end. McClair's party will have to stay aboard for the rest of the trip and come back here with you."

Jewell glanced at McClair with some satisfaction. At least the man was only a junior officer; he had no intention of sacrificing his bunk for an army captain.

"When will the stores come aboard, sir ?" he asked.

"Tomorrow, then you sail on the following day—the 27th. I'll give you your sailing orders tomorrow evening."

With a slight nod, Fawkes indicated he was busy and the two officers left, McClair promising to return the next day to help in loading the equipment. With him would be his party— Captain A. Croft of the Inshore Special Service Unit, and Sergeant J. Thompson of the Special Boat Section, Combined Operations.

Next day the three soldiers reported aboard, a steady stream of crates and sacks following, to be stowed away below. Apart from the Commandos, only Jewell knew that the stores consisted of two-way radio transmitters and receivers, stens, machine-guns, pistols, signal lamps, ammunition, grenades and containers of special explosives for sabotage. He shuddered slightly when McClair pointed to one case vanishing down the fore hatch and muttered:

"That's a good one for 'em. Full of killing knives sharper than razors and as light as stilettos. Have enormous amount of fun with those little darlings."

No doubt about it, thought Jewell, these chaps are just as bloodthirsty as the Jumbo Courtney trio. They might do anything once they got ashore; after all it was unthinkable for a Commando to leave enemy territory without collecting at least one scalp. Whatever lay ahead on this trip, it was probably going to be anything but dull.

CHAPTER THIRTEEN

OPERATION BURROW

SERAPH sailed into the Mediterranean on August 27th with a fair wind and sea causing her lean shape to plunge forward in a sliding roll. Her bows were under water, riding through it, and the foaming waves swished down her sides to loose themselves in the thin wake churned from her propellers. There was an air of renewed energy and keen anticipation among the crew who looked forward to this adventure of gun-running behind enemy lines.

The passage into the Tyrrhenian Sea was undisturbed, although two aircraft sightings through the periscope sent *Seraph* into the depths where there was no risk of an inquisitive pilot sighting her grey-black shape outlined beneath the blue surface of the sea. On the 31st the Italian mainland came over the horizon.

McClair joined Jewell on the bridge that evening after dark and said softly: "I'd like to have a look at some of the bays around here. How about starting by the Portofino promontory ?"

Jewell nodded. They decided to consult the navigator and his charts, but when Davis met them in the control room he introduced a sour note.

"Well, sir, I suppose you know an enemy minefield has been reported right along this coast." Jewell didn't.

McClair whitened. "Can't be helped," he said. "We promised these Italians we would 'cache' the stuff somewhere in there." He stabbed a finger at the coastline on the chart.

Jewell shrugged. "O.K. if that's where you want to go, that's where we'll take you."

Curiously the long absence of any American influence aboard had caused a lapse in the use of slang. There was little fun in it unless someone of the "North Africa Canoeists Club" was around to be amused or irritated. Wright and Gaylord had enjoyed the slang more than the others and had managed to master it by introducing a certain British element into their natural American accents.

Jewell grinned to himself at the thought and rather unfairly compared the serious young McClair, who tended to use an exaggerated form of the traditional English understatement, with the calm, easy informality and unconcern of the Americans they had come to know so well.

Davis warned him they were nearing the suspected minefield and he automatically remembered the rules by which the submarine war was played—the most important being to dive deep under a minefield and stay deep until you were certain the roof was clear. *Seraph* dived to 200 feet. The asdic operator switched on the mine detector unit which beamed above, below and ahead to give warning of the many-horned iron spheres which had claimed so many of her sister submarines.

At two knots, she crept ahead. Inside, the crew's mood changed as the word passed from one compartment to another that they were entering a minefield.

Jewell pulled a magazine from behind an instrument panel and sat down to read; Edsell bent intently over the chart table; Scott stood by the fore and after hydroplane operators ready to act instantly should the detector react to a mine. In the for'ard torpedo room there was silence. These men could not but sense that if the bows were blown in they had very little hope of survival. Of the soldiers Sergeant Thompson seemed the most at ease. Always cleaning knives, guns or leather belts, he had become a favourite among the crew who had made him an honorary member of the mess deck.

Edsell broke the silence. "We've been going an hour now, sir. Bottom's beginning to slope a little from the fifty fathom mark."

"Right. Let's go up to 150 feet, Number One."

The heavy muggy air, coupled with the tension, produced a sweatiness which grew worse as time forced itself round the clock until another hour had passed.

"Cross the thirty fathom mark now, sir, and bottom slopes a little quicker from here on," reminded Edsell.

Jewell looked up from his magazine. "How much longer before we clear this minefield?"

"About another forty minutes, sir."

"Take her up to 100 feet, Number One."

A slight bump thudded through the submarine. Eyes swung

round, stomachs knotted. Nothing happened. Whatever it had been, *Seraph* had shaken herself clear.

Now there were more glances at the clock. The word had spread that Lieutenant Edsell had estimated forty minutes before they were clear. Not long now.

Suddenly, Edsell unbent and announced cheerfully, "We're clear, sir, and I think we ought to go up. Frankly," he grinned in mock astonishment, "I'm surprised we haven't touched bottom. Only a couple of miles off the coast now, or should be."

Soft chatter broke out and a few experimental bangs were heard as men tested their nerves. When they found the noise no longer startled them, they began chuckling with relief.

Jewell could see nothing threatening through the periscope, the asdic operator found no evidence of shipping in the neighbourhood, so *Seraph* surfaced, drained the water from her back and settled down on even keel. The watch and the soldiers climbed to the bridge to see how accurate Edsell's navigation had been. Too good, thought Jewell, as he altered course away from the coastline little more than half a mile away.

For the next hour *Seraph* prowled the tiny bays and coves searching for one which suited McClair's perfectionist mind. This was a tiny cove marked on the chart as Casa Dell-Oro. When he had finished sweeping the hilly background to the beach with his binoculars, McClair at last announced the journey's end. Here they would bury the treasure store of arms as ordered in OPERATION BURROW.

Seraph withdrew to seaward while the boats were brought out on deck, but the exercise was soon interrupted when a look-out sighted several darkened shapes approaching from the south. Back down the fore hatch went the boats and quickly she vanished from sight. It was a convoy of two small merchant ships escorted by two destroyers. *Seraph* was ideally placed for an attack but, to his chagrin, Jewell had to let the enemy pass unmolested. An attack at that stage might only compromise the purpose of their visit to this coast—the arms "cache".

When the convoy had passed into the night, she surfaced again and moved towards the shore, coming to stop inside the cove about 300 yards from the beach. The Commandos had brought two boats—a folbot and a self-inflating rubber dinghy similar to those used by the R.A.F. It promised to be a difficult operation as *Seraph* was rolling heavily in a ground swell.

The folbot was launched first and immediately capsized in the swell, as had been feared, and all efforts were now concentrated on the rubber dinghy. It could be inflated by hand pump or by releasing a bottle of carbon dioxide attached to its side. As the latter might be needed urgently in an emergency ashore, the hand pump was used on the fore deck. Once launched it rode the swell comfortably and was quickly loaded with the precious stores for the guerillas. An astonishing weight in guns, ammunition and radio sets rode safely in the dinghy. When it appeared likely to fold up and sink, the three soldiers jumped in, waved and paddled away towards the beach. *Seraph* went astern out of the cove, turned to seaward and submerged out of sight in case there should be alert guards in the neighbourhood.

The Commandos found the beach; what there was of it offered little assistance in getting ashore. More rocks than sand, and the heavy surf made the safety of boat and stores uncertain. Before reaching the surf, McClair leaped out and waded ashore to reconnoitre the beach and cliffs.

Twenty-five yards inland he found a thick barbed wire barrier running along the coast and a few yards the other side a guard hut showing a light. He hurried back to the beach in a crouching run, signalled the boat and waded out to steady it as the surf took hold and threatened to toss the valuable cargo overboard.

A few minutes later it was beached and the stores were being stacked behind some rocks. The light still shone from the guard hut only 50 yards away. It was a still night with little wind, and every sound carried. Dressed in overalls and rubber-soled slippers the Commandos merely scuffled as they placed each crate carefully on the ground. A rattling stone, an uncontrolled cough or sneeze, a stumble against a rock or bush, and the guards would come running to investigate.

Working silently with hand signs to do their talking the soldiers had the boat emptied in a few minutes and crawled back to the barbed wire entanglement. Sergeant Thompson drew a pair of wire cutters from his pocket and, while the two officers held each strand of wire to avoid flip-backs, he clipped a gap 4 feet high and 3 across.

They had worked together as a team doing this sort of thing many times before and it was accomplished deftly and without noise. First through was Croft who ran up to the hut, listened, and ran down to the left. About 20 yards from the hut he found a bush growing by itself among the rocks and easily recognisable to the partisans who would come one night armed with spades to dig up the stores.

Then he returned to the gap in the wire, reported by signs to McClair and took Thompson back to the beach to help carry the crates up to the bush. For the next hour the three damp but sweating soldiers dug into the ground, cursing to themselves when they struck slate and rock. By the time the hole was deep enough to satisfy their exacting standards, it was past 1 a.m.

McClair beckoned to his companions who continued with the burial while he moved up to the guard hut to listen by the lighted window for a moment before disappearing into the rocks behind. Ten minutes later he emerged from the shadows to confirm by signs that there were no other guards and assisted in replacing the earth over the stones. Not a pebble rolled away to arouse suspicion in the hut; not a branch of the bush was touched, not a twig broken underfoot to crack a warning of intruders.

Suddenly the door of the hut creaked; the Commandos froze. A voice drifted gutturally across the 20 yards separating OPERATION BURROW from the guards. McClair peeked round the bush and saw a German sentry put on his helmet and start walking—towards them. He ducked back and closed a hand over his knife. Seeing the gesture, his companions drew their own very slowly.

They counted his paces ... eleven ... twelve ... thirteen ... fourteen ... fifteen ... five more steps and he would be on top of them. At nineteen paces he stopped, less than a yard away. The bush swayed as he leant his sub-machine gun against it. He cleared his throat and spat at a spot only inches from Thompson's hunched figure. This was followed by an unexpected development; he relieved himself into the bush. With remarkable self-control McClair remained rigid and his companions, disciplined to obey in tight corners, followed his example.

The awful experience was soon over and, with a grunt, the German picked up his gun and moved away—this time towards the gap in the barbed wire. Rapidly the soldiers carried on patting down the soil over the burial ground and removing all signs of their presence. With that done, they were ready to silence the zealous guard. Their luck held. The German turned away from the fence a few yards before he was close enough to see their handiwork and after a long look out at sea, returned to the hut and was last seen closing the door behind him.

McClair sighed with relief. He had not wanted to kill that night as any untoward event at the spot would arouse suspicion and alert the Germans that a landing had been made. The Italian guerillas would end the worries of those guards the night they came for the cached equipment.

Once they had returned through the gap in the barbed wire, there was another important chore—each strand of cut wire had to be rejoined and made to look as undisturbed as possible. The joins would have to be good enough to remain unnoticed for at least forty-eight hours. Once again training made it comparatively simple for these three young intruders who were soon back on the rocky beach carefully obliterating their footsteps by brushing a dead branch over the sand behind them.

They had some trouble in persuading the rubber dinghy to stay right side up in the surf but, after several anxious moments, the three were settled in, over the surf and out into the calm swell. By the time they passed through the entrance of the cove and looked back, the light in the guard hut had vanished behind a hill.

Seraph was on the surface waiting for their return. Breathing heavily, the trio were dragged inboard and taken below for a rub-down and glasses of brandy. David Scott deflated the rubber dinghy and manhandled it down through the conning tower hatch. Halfway down it jammed and in trying to free it the toggle of the carbon dioxide bottle caught on a jagged piece of metal. The stopper came out with a faint hiss. In seconds Scott was gassed, his struggles to come up for air growing feebler until he subsided into unconsciousness. Jewell wrote in his report of proceedings:

"We heard a faint commotion going on in the tower hatch and looked down to see the First Lieutenant temporarily asphyxiated by the accidental release of the dinghy's self-inflation device. We pulled him up to the bridge, had the offending boat removed and stowed away and then turned to see what could be done about Lieutenant Scott. Fresh air was his cure and after a minute or two, his eyes blinked open and he climbed slowly to his feet completely unaware of what had happened."

After this incident, *Seraph* turned seawards and dived towards the minefield—she would have to pass through it again to clear the coastline into open sea. Once again the crew and their passengers would have to suffer the agonising suspense of three hours waiting while *Seraph* nosed her way clear of danger. She had been lucky the first time but there was a limit to luck. Before dawn, however, they were safely into the Tyrrhenian Sea to begin seeking out the enemy. Operation Burrow had been successfully completed and another symbol would appear on her Jolly Roger when *Seraph* next entered harbour.

With dawn approaching rapidly, she was preparing for the morning dive. Supper had been served and the dishes cleared; smokers had thrown away their last cigarette stubs and the bridge personnel had taken their last gulps of fresh air for the next twelve hours. From the west appeared the dark shapes of ships. Startled, *Seraph* dived and looked at them from the hidden vantage point of periscope depth. It was an E-boat obviously on anti-submarine sweep. Hoping she had not been seen, *Seraph* crept past her, glancing back every few seconds to satisfy herself she was not being followed. At 10 a.m. a second E-boat, accompanied by a schooner, joined the first. There was considerable flashing of signal lights and the first hunter departed with the schooner leaving the second to continue the search. This was sufficient activity to arouse speculation as to whether the Commandos had left some trace ashore of their operations. Then the E-boat began dropping depth charges in a line, luckily away from *Seraph*.

By midday, the enemy was obviously bored with duties or had completed the pattern of firing, for he picked up speed and headed for the Portofino point.

At 6 p.m. yet another E-boat appeared, intent on maintaining the hunt and, reluctantly, *Seraph* moved away from the hunting ground to less crowded waters where she could surface and dispatch her report to Algiers.

Transmitting began at 10.30 p.m. but the long message, including the Commando report for Combined Operations headquarters and the exact location of the burial ground, took until five in the morning to clear. Captain McClair's report brilliantly understated his exploit: "After landing on a rocky beach at Casa Dell-Oro," he said, "I went ashore and the dinghy lay off while I made a reconnaissance. I encountered barbed wire defences about 25 yards inland. These were easily penetrated and just up the hill was a hut in which there was a light very poorly blacked out. We then brought the dinghy and stores ashore—this being a little difficult owing to the swell and rocks and it is doubtful if it would have been at all possible had we brought the folbot.

"Captain Croft reconnoitred to select a site for burying the stores and chose a large bush 20 yards from the hut. I had already considered it unlikely that a fisherman or shepherd would have a light on at that hour and thought it to be inhabited by inefficient guards.

"While Captain Croft and Sergeant Thompson commenced work I made a further reconnaissance to make sure there were no more sentries around and returned to assist them. The secreting of the stores was carried out very quickly and all traces of our work carefully removed. Although we were once disturbed I have every reason to believe the enemy will not suspect a landing has been made.

"I must emphasise how impressed I was with the behaviour of the rubber dinghy and I suggest any future operations involving the landing of stores should be done by dinghy.

"Great co-operation and consideration shown throughout 'Burrow' by Captain and crew of *Seraph*."

It was a relief to get the signal over, knowing that it would be routed through Captain Fawkes and Combined Operations to the partisans who would be already sharpening their spades in anticipation. *Seraph* made her way to the northern tip of Corsica where it was hoped targets would abound.

At 1.35 p.m. on September 2nd she made contact with two

large merchantmen of about 6,000 tons each escorted by two E-boats.

Jewell wrote later: "Those fellows were masters of evasive tactics. They had not seen anything or had any warning that we were in the vicinity but they zigzagged as much as sixty degrees off their course every few minutes. I had never seen anything quite like this before."

The cargo ships were travelling light in ballast. *Seraph* lined her sights and lifted her bows slightly as the torpedo shot away at the leading ship. Jewell had done his best to estimate the rate and timing of the enemy zigzag, but to his consternation the target altered course towards *Seraph* just as he fired. It was an infuriating miss and she dived away, only too well aware that it would not be long before the torpedo tracks were sighted and the E-boats came to plaster the area with depth charges.

By now McClair, Croft and Thompson were becoming accustomed to submarine life and these torpedo attacks were a novel, exciting experience for them. McClair voiced his disappointment that they were not going to have another shot at this convoy and Jewell sighed heavily. These three were as bad as Courtney, Livingstone and Foote. They would not be happy until *Seraph* had drawn blood—perhaps to compensate for their own inability to scalp the sentry ashore.

Seraph headed now for Bastia, a busy Corsican port teeming with potential targets, and at dawn on the 3rd she reached a patrol line some five miles outside the harbour entrance. It was calm, slightly misty with no wind.

Not long after 8 a.m., two deeply-laden supply ships escorted by an "Abba" class destroyer and an E-boat came steaming towards *Seraph*'s submerged position. She moved across to an attacking station and Jewell, standing crouched at the periscope with a tacky film of oil and water under his feet and drops of sea water trickling from the periscope column on to his head, brought the sights to bear. The attack team— Scott, Norris, Edsell, the telegraphists, hydroplane operators and helmsman—watched and waited for his orders. Only he knew what was taking place on the surface. He called out the range and bearing; then . . . "Fire Numbers One, Two, Three and Four."

Lights flashed in the torpedo room and the four torpedoes

Seraph signposted the way to Sicily for the U.S. Seventh Army. General George Patton directs beach operations in Sicily with General Theodore Roosevelt (*left*), son of a former President.

Rosemary Galloway.

Kay Summersby, General Eisenhower's driver.

Combined American and British Guard of Honour salute Admiral Sir Andrew Cunningham when he relinquished his command in 1943. He is seen here with General Eisenhower and Vice-Admiral Hewitt of the U.S. Navy.

hurtled from the bows. The periscope came down with a loud hiss and they waited for the explosions. There was not long to wait: Jewell had forgotten they were in shallow water with sand and mud banks stretching out from the coast. The first torpedo had travelled little more than 200 yards when it exploded on a sandbank. The other three ran aground and exploded a few seconds later causing *Seraph* to leap about like a porpoise. The crew were thrown around while Scott tried desperately to regain trim. Eventually the ballast tanks were flooded drastically and, groaning under the vast weight of sea water, she abruptly stopped her jumping to plunge downwards. She hit bottom and stuck in the mud at 110 feet. Her movements steadied, the crew picked themselves up to take stock of their position. The explosions and *Seraph*'s porpoise-like appearances on the surface would set off a hunt. Now they were stuck in the mud, not nearly as deep as they would have liked. With the position known it seemed unlikely that the enemy could miss.

The first pattern of depth charges fell some way off but soon an additional escort rushed from Bastia to join the hunt picked up the immobile submarine on his asdic. He brought his partners to the spot and the subsequent deluge was the prelude to the worst and most drastic bombing of *Seraph*'s career. Jewell ordered all machinery and movement stopped for silent routine.

The next two patterns came down accurately but fell across the submarine without actually hitting her. The noise inside was deafening and the boat shuddered under the pounding with seams creaking in protest at the strain imposed on the rivets. Jewell cocked his head as another roar announced the next barrage. Another series of crashes and the submarine was jerked violently about the sea bed. But there was a glint of triumph on Jewell's face. Those last three patterns of charges had been close enough to blow their sides in but, miraculously, *Seraph* still lived.

The mud which held them trapped was also saving their lives. The depth charges were tumbling into the mud before exploding and several feet of it were acting as shock absorbers. Submariners become fatalistic about depth charging; the stuffiness of bad air also makes it easy to sleep soundly. At this moment of extreme danger, some turned in including the

L

newly-joined Lieutenant Harris. Meanwhile, the helmsman was calmly chalking up the number of depth charges on a slate.

Another clatter announced the next pattern; and suddenly *Seraph* trembled. At least one depth charge had landed on the fore deck. A few seconds passed and they could hear it slowly roll down the casing. The submarine lurched and the noise of rolling stopped. There was silence and everyone waited tensely for the explosion which would blast in the deck and be followed by an inrush of water. A rating in the control room turned towards Jewell, and his soft-spoken plea made half in earnest echoed loudly through the hull: "Let's do some praying, sir. Or will you read the burial service?" His mates were slightly shocked that anyone should speak. *Seraph*'s stern settled lower and the rolling above on the fore deck began again as the depth charge gathered speed. Jewell grinned back at the sailor. "You haven't prayed for years. You should have thought about a time like this long ago. Can't think why God should help you now." He looked back at the magazine and appeared to continue his reading.

Above there came a sudden thump as the depth charge hit the conning tower. A few more slight crunches and they could hear it roll over the side to land with a slight thud in the mud.

Seraph leaned over as though in a high wind as the roar of an explosion deafened her crew. Lights faltered and went out. The sound of breaking glass, smashing crockery, and the metallic clang of twisted instruments and valves blended with the noise outside, plucking at threadbare nerves.

Suddenly it was over and the submarine struggled to regain her balance, slowly righting herself with a long shuddering effort. It seemed impossible that her hull could have withstood the concussion but forty-four men paid silent tribute then to her builders, Vickers-Armstrongs, whose shipyard had been the cradle for the tough and dependable veteran.

Her inside was an appalling sight; everything breakable had been smashed and the pieces cluttered up the living space. The magnetic compass had broken down so there was no way of knowing in which direction they were pointing until the gyro could be brought into use by starting up the generators again.

The explosion had torn *Seraph* loose from the mud and blown her up to 90 feet despite the weight of water pressing down above her. Ballast tanks were pumped out and Scott regained a reasonable trim. The electric motors hummed back to life, the magnetic compass was stripped and fixed and the gyro slipped into gear. Jewell decided to take her up for a look; anything was better than being a sitting target on the bottom. At least they could now take some evasive action. She levelled off at 30 feet, the periscope was raised with Jewell bending over the eyepieces. He had been looking forward to seeing the world outside, but he saw little enough of it. Instead he almost shouted: "Down periscope." The "window" had been filled by the side of an enemy destroyer lying stopped trying to regain asdic contact with the submarine. *Seraph* pointed her stern at the ambusher and carefully, if hurriedly, made off from the scene with the periscope going up and down anxiously. It was another miracle that she was not picked up by the destroyer; even the Commandos were learning to become fatalistic and accept phenomena which gave submariners so much excitement.

Now that they were safe, the three soldiers chattered away in high delight at the experience. They had been shaken and not a little scared, like all the others, but they had a story to take back to Combined Operations headquarters which few Army men could equal.

Scott and Stevenson prowled on inspection. The seams had held and the principal mechanism seemed to have escaped serious damage. They suspected that the torpedo tubes had been distorted but how much would not be known until another attack was made.

A yawning face staggered past Jewell in the control room. He remembered then that Harris had turned in when the depth charges started falling. Surely he could not have slept through it all!

"Where have you been, Harris? In your bunk all the time?"

"Just woke up, sir. Damn glad we're on the move again, though. Seems to be a lot of damage inside here. Were we bombed much, sir?" Unbelievably, he had slept soundly throughout the worst depth charging he was likely to survive.

Running repairs completed, *Seraph* sailed towards the

Italian coast to continue her patrol. Corsica would be a good place to stay away from just for the present. The crew had emerged from the underwater torment with the self-confidence of a team which had survived the worst any opponent could offer. But *Seraph* had taken tremendous punishment and first aid patching could be only a temporary expedient. She needed professional attention for at least ten major defects and a general overhaul to recover her former buoyancy—if she ever would.

At 3 a.m. on the 9th when lunch had been cleared away from the Wardroom a signal was received from the Commander-in-Chief forbidding any future attacks on Italian cruisers and destroyers. The officers beamed at this first indication of a crack in enemy resistance. Their speculation proved accurate two hours later when an additional signal announced the Italian surrender.

But this would not mean an end to the submarine war. The Germans were to stay in Italy and use the coastal waters for transporting supplies and troops—mostly in Italian ships. It was not long before the first Germans came in sight.

CHAPTER FOURTEEN

SURFACE ACTIONS

THE signal from Algiers told all submarines to intercept Italian ships and divert them to Allied ports in North Africa or to Malta.

By now *Seraph* had reached the Troja Island area and, throughout the 9th, sighted large numbers of small craft and destroyers heading northwards. Mostly they presented little in the way of targets, being too far away, too small or too fast. In the early afternooon it was felt necessary to interrupt all this hurried coming and going by stopping an Italian coaster. It felt strange to surface under the brilliant sun in enemy waters known to be overcrowded with all sorts of lethal traps for British submarines. *Seraph* fired two shots across the coaster's bows as a warning to stop, and closed alongside.

In answer to a shout, the skipper replied that he was the *Janus* bound for Italy with a cargo of iron ore. Not yet accustomed to this chatting with an ex-enemy while surfaced on a sunny day, *Seraph* was not prepared to take the skipper's word. A boarding party was sent across, found there were no Germans aboard, that she was indeed carrying iron ore and seemed in all respects to be truthful. Further questioning revealed that she had been loaded in Corsica and, having received no orders from the German authorities, had set out on her own to deliver the ore to its destination, Genoa.

Genoa was in German hands and Jewell suggested that the skipper might try a more acceptable port such as one in North Africa. The Italian was quick to realise his predicament and gladly agreed to alter course. He was instructed to head for Algiers where he would be met outside, escorted in and put to work for the Allies. Work meant money and the chance of continuity in the supply of this commodity caused him to beam with undisguised pleasure.

Half an hour later, the iron ore vanished over *Seraph*'s horizon heading for Allied munition factories.

There was little doubt in all their minds that the defeat of

Italy had revolutionised the submarine war in the Mediterranean. The rules had laid down that it was bad insurance to surface by day anywhere near the Italian coast or its islands and offshoots. But the rules—or this one at any rate—were now clearly in need of amendment. New ones would have to be devised in the same manner as the old—by practical experience.

At 7.19 a.m. next day, while still on the surface when she would have been dived normally, *Seraph* sighted an interesting target—two large German gunboats, known as "R" boats—steaming down one side of Troja Island, one towing the other. She sailed along the opposite side and waited at the tip of the island to greet them. The 3-inch gun's crew were closed up at action stations and, at Jewell's command to fire, the gun barked viciously making *Seraph* jump almost as much as the Germans. The gun had rarely been fired in anger before—a graphic illustration of changing times in the Mediterranean.

The first three rounds fell short, the fourth over the leading gunboat. The enemy replied half-heartedly and two small-calibre shells sent up spurts of water fifty yards short of *Seraph*. After her sixth salvo a look-out spotted a formation of five aircraft in the sun wheeling round to dive. Klaxons sounded and *Seraph* dived rapidly, Jewell taking time before closing the "lid" to identify the attackers as F.W.187s—distinctly efficient and unpleasant Focke Wolff fighter-bombers.

She made her way back to the north-west corner of Troja Island to wait at periscope depth for more enemy traffic to appear and, sure enough, some three hours later, the previous engagement looked like being repeated. Two more large gunboats, the first towing the second, steamed into the narrow passage separating the island from the mainland. *Seraph* surfaced, slipped quickly down the seaward side, closed up the gun's crews and sat in wait at the other end.

The brace of slow-moving targets soon hove in sight. This time she fired at the second gunboat and scored a direct hit with her second shot. The enemy began burning furiously. The first gunboat replied with vigour, but *Seraph* sailed in towards her presenting a tiny end-on target while she shelled the German with satisfactory accuracy. This manœuvre with a submarine taking the initiative from a gun-boat and actually steaming in on the surface to join action unnerved the enemy gunners who had never before experienced such tactics. Their aim was wild and soon the gunboat was hit repeatedly and caught fire. The German crews, demoralised by *Seraph*'s spirited attack, jumped overboard and swam furiously for the island where Italian peasants, who had crowded to the beach to watch the action, cheered frantically and prepared to meet their former allies with hoots of derision.

The two gunboats burned heavily for nearly an hour before they disintegrated slowly under the impact of exploding ammunition and finally sank.

The sea was still boiling over the last remains of the second to go down when another convoy came in sight from the Troja Island passage—eight tank-landing craft escorted by three "R" boats. This was too strong a force for *Seraph*'s 3-inch gun to handle and too small for torpedo attack. They were all shallow-draught vessels and the torpedoes would be more likely than not to run beneath them.

Seraph dived out of the way and reluctantly allowed the enemy unmolested passage. For the large part of the day a whole stream of landing craft, huge barges and gunboats came through the narrow straits in numbers too powerful to attack.

Her patient wait ended at 4.45 p.m. when two large transport barges, well down in the water under heavy loads, were sighted approaching the northern entrance. She surfaced, and the 3-inch gun belched into action engaging the leading transport. The enemy, equipped with light machine-guns, replied gallantly and there were several uncomfortable minutes on the bridge before Jewell shouted at the gun's crew:

"For heaven's sake, hit the damn things."

Obligingly, the leading barge was hit amidships with the next salvo and black smoke began pouring from its holds. Cheers echoed faintly from the islanders, but were drowned almost instantly by a tremendous explosion as the burning barge vanished in a sudden burst of flame and smoke. There was no sign of her crew abandoning ship and it seemed likely they had been blown up as well. A curious German aircraft dived to see what was happening and *Seraph* quickly submerged.

Ten minutes later she surfaced again only to find that the second barge had crammed on speed in an attempt to use the aircraft's intervention to run away. The result was that he could still be hit by *Seraph* who was outside the range of his own lighter armament. Grasping this advantage, the gunners set about destroying the enemy with a punishingly accurate fire. The barge turned back towards the island to seek shelter on its other side but, before getting very far, two hits on the stern so frightened the crew that they beached the barge, scrambled ashore and headed inland as fast as they could run. *Seraph* approached the target to demolish it without unnecessary waste of ammunition, but six more rounds of 3-inch failed to set it alight and Norris, the Gunnery Officer, reported their ammunition expended.

Jewell ordered him to fire starshell into the barge which had to be destroyed before they left the area. Six rounds failed to achieve any noticeable result and *Seraph* closed as near as possible to send a demolition party aboard. Suddenly, a menacing column of black smoke poured from one of the hatch covers and, recognising the symptoms, she withdrew hurriedly to avoid being blown up herself in the thundering explosion that wrecked the beached barge. The gun action had lasted for two hours and was the longest in *Seraph*'s life.

After dark on the surface, radio silence was broken to inform *Maidstone* that her ammunition had been expended; the reply ordered her to return to base on the 12th—another two days. There was time for at least one more engagement and it came after dawn, north of Troja Island, when a large Kriegstransporter, a curiously designed barge-like affair specially produced to supply Rommel's Afrika Corps, came in sight escorted by two E-boats. These last were the pests of Allied submarines, infesting the Mediterranean in large numbers and causing untold trouble and damage. They were dangerous opponents, deadly in anti-submarine work and against our inshore supply convoys. There would be no regrets among submariners generally when these warships were removed altogether from the theatre.

Seraph approached her target at periscope depth for a submerged torpedo attack. She manœuvred into a perfect attack position, Jewell's estimation of the Kriegstransporter's course and speed being reasonably accurate and conditions about as good as they could be for a submarine.

Three torpedoes were fired, one veering away wildly to miss the nearest E-boat which sighted its track and altered course towards *Seraph*. She went down deep and had reached 100 feet when the sound of two more explosions ripped faintly through the water, time checks showing that they coincided with the correct runs of the other two torpedoes. They could have hit the transporter.

Further speculation was cut short by the familiar tumbling roar of the depth charges. They were accurately placed, but this time *Seraph* was able to take evasive action. Nevertheless, the next two hours were not pleasant as she twisted and turned to avoid well-directed attacks and cleverly-aimed patterns of charges. Once again she took a severe hammering, but nothing like as furious as that off Bastia. There was time for Scott and Norris to investigate the reason for the first torpedo's briefly erratic career and they reported that the previous depth charging had almost certainly damaged the tubes. No doubt the torpedoes had been unsettled at the shaking they had taken earlier that day.

Forty minutes later the E-boats were heard departing and *Seraph* came up for a look. Black smoke was pouring from the other side of the island, a sign that at least one torpedo had hit the transport and her escorts were taking her limping body back to harbour. There was no chance of catching up with them to find out, so she lay in wait for something more spectacular to appear.

It was not yet noon when a small merchantman arrived escorted by the inevitable E-boat. They came into the periscope sights at close range. Jewell fired only one torpedo this time and it hit the merchant ship amidships. She leaped out of the water under the explosive impact and settled back, a blazing wreck. *Seraph* ducked away to avoid the escort's search, but came up again half an hour later in time to witness the death throes of the coaster which sank slowly with its bows pointing up at the sky. The E-boat was nearby, picking up survivors and, taking advantage of this pre-occupation, *Seraph* left the battlefield.

At last her patient patrolling had been rewarded by something more substantial than supply barges. This would add at least another 2,000 tons to her score.

To comply with Captain Fawkes's order to return to base on the 12th, *Seraph* sailed down the Italian coast in search of prey but, sighting nothing, turned off for Algiers at dusk and arrived off the harbour entrance with the Jolly Roger flying at dawn. She was tied up in time for breakfast and Jewell reported to Fawkes on board *Maidstone* where they discussed his Report of Proceedings over coffee.

It had not been the most rewarding trip in their Mediterranean service, but Fawkes was not surprised by the lack of large targets; other submarines had also reported sighting little besides transport barges.

"That is only to be expected," he commented. "Now that the Italians are out, the Germans have very little shipping left in this part of the world except the specially-designed stuff they sent down to keep Rommel supplied. I'm afraid we are really going to have to hunt hard for targets from now on."

Seraph was tired, suffering from at least ten major wounds and no longer behaving like the lithe active youngster who had first appeared in the Mediterranean nearly eighteen months before. Now she needed time to rest and recover from the scars of her agonising hours off Bastia. *Maidstone*'s repair crews descended upon her and set about making good her damage in preparation for the next patrol. With the enemy on the defensive it was important that his shipping should be harried and swept from the sea quickly and certainly.

This meant that *Seraph*'s defects were only temporarily repaired and, by the first week in October, she was ready for sea again. The crew had replenished depleted stocks of American tinned food by surreptitious raids on the dockyard supply dump; the Red Cross nurses had loaded them down with sweets. On October 2nd, Captain Fawkes came aboard to wish them well on their next patrol off Toulon, where the Germans were strengthening the southern French defences against possible invasion.

On the 3rd, she was surfaced in the evening before dusk when a flight of Wellington bombers circled her in case she proved to be a lost U-boat. Recognition signals were exchanged and the airmen carried out several dummy bombing runs to relieve the monotony.

Next day, she moved close inshore at periscope depth in an attempt to intercept anything small that might be hugging the coastline. It was a sentimental journey for this was the stretch of coast from which Giraud had been rescued and the crew wondered vaguely about the fate which might have befallen the fisherman who had so expertly handled his boat that stormy night.

Nothing was sighted that day until after darkness when they received a signal from Captain (S) 8. It was an order to make all possible speed back to Algiers—an unexpected order as submarines were rarely recalled from patrols after little more than twenty-four hours. *Seraph* was not sorry; the hasty repairs to her wounds had been so hurried that they were cracking open again.

She headed for North Africa speculating on her future. There could be but one reason for her recall—transfer to another theatre of operations. For some weeks there had been talk in *Maidstone* of the Flotilla moving to the Far East. The need for a large force of submarines in the Middle East had fallen away; the flotillas at home were quite capable of dealing with the enemy in the North Sea; and the only sea power ranged against the Allies in any strength was Japan. It was generally agreed that this prospect offered no future at all for the weary *Seraph*.

They were to discover that the enemy could still bite in the western Mediterranean. At midnight on the 5th when the crew were relaxed and gloomily foreseeing events in faraway places, a red stream of tracer bullets shot from the misty darkness across their bows. A surfaced U-boat came in sight still shooting a little wildly. Jewell indignantly turned her on to a firing course, but the enemy dived as he was about to retaliate. *Seraph* followed suit in double quick time, accepting the challenge of an underwater duel.

This was a favourite sport of U-boats when they encountered Allied submarines; they threw down the glove on sighting and dived to a submarine's equivalent of the usual ten paces. With the challenge answered, both submarines stalked each other in the darkness below the surface.

The careful hunt which might end in collision at any moment continued for an hour until, tiring of the sport, *Seraph* surfaced and resumed her passage home. The sea was rising quickly and she had lost her former bounce in this sort of weather. No longer filled with the vitality of early youth she forced her way through the choppy sea with the pumping, pounding thrust of a tiring racehorse straining to reach the winning post.

She was to receive little sympathy from *Maidstone*. Once berthed alongside, Jewell sought Captain Fawkes to learn the reason for their recall and found their guesses well clear of the mark. The Germans were expected at any day to launch an invasion of several important Dodecanese Islands in the Aegean. The submarine flotillas were to reinforce the eastern Mediterranean and sink the invasion force while still at sea.

The Commander-in-Chief's review of the submarine war said: "The march of events in the Mediterranean and the demands of other theatres call for a change in submarine dispositions and policy. The situation now developing leaves only two useful areas of submarine operations—the Gulf of Genoa and the Aegean. A third area in the Adriatic may ultimately prove to have some importance.

"In view of this appreciation, the 'S' class of the Eighth Flotilla should be transferred to the eastern Mediterranean for operations in the Aegean where it is likely the enemy is preparing to occupy the Dodecanese. It is desirable that in this event, his invasion fleet should be destroyed before reaching its destination."

From Captain Fawkes, Jewell learned that Eisenhower's attempt to decorate *Seraph* had failed. Congress had no precedent for this and President Roosevelt had suggested it would be more diplomatic if the General found some other way.

Fawkes also told Jewell to arrange for transferring to the Beirut command, but before *Seraph* could prepare for sea she was alerted for a trip to Corsica. French forces had landed on the island and were quickly proving, under Giraud, that they were capable of defeating the Germans.

Attached to Giraud's staff and acting as an advance scout was an American army officer, Major-General Robert Peake, who maintained liaison between Eisenhower, Giraud and the French field commander, General Martin. In a message to the Supreme Commander, Peake had said:

"I am getting involved with a small British colony and one United States citizen here. They are destitute and the two elderly English ladies have just been released from a concentration camp. I am advancing them money to buy food and clothing as otherwise they might starve. I suggest they are taken to North Africa or Gibraltar and, with the American citizen, flown to England."

Eisenhower was so used to passing pick-up trips to the submarines that this one automatically came to Captain Fawkes who, for the life of him, could not quite see why a submarine was required when an ordinary supply ship or aircraft could do the job. He submitted the request from Allied Headquarters to Admiral Cunningham and ordered *Seraph* to prepare for a voyage to Corsica in case "ABC" approved. But he did not approve and *Seraph* relaxed to continue packing up all the odds and ends she had collected in a year of operating from Algiers.

There were so many people who wanted to say goodbye and wish her luck—Rosemary Galloway, Kay Summersby, the Red Cross nurses, Private Bocciccio from Brooklyn whom the Fifth Army, then in Italy, had left behind with *Maidstone*, and finally Captain Fawkes and the depot ship's staff officers who had done so much for *Seraph* when she most needed help. Ashore in the new city, up the hill in the old walled town and along the Kasbah there were also many obscure nameless people who had befriended some of the more adventurous sailors and had to be visited for the last time.

When a ship has served under one command and operated from one base throughout a dangerous and uncertain period there are many debts to leave behind when she moves—debts of kindness and generosity which can never be repaid.

Seraph sailed regretfully from Algiers. Throughout the uneventful passage to Beirut, the crew lavished care and attention on her, oiling, greasing and mending groaning joints and broken mechanism. She was still their only link with safety, and plenty of action was waiting for her next venture to sea on an operational patrol. There were also fourteen German soldiers unwittingly sailing to meet her.

CHAPTER FIFTEEN

THE LAST PATROL

A T the outbreak of war the Dodecanese were owned and occupied by the Italians. A small group had been captured by the Allies and, at the first sign of Italian defection, the Germans had taken over another large number. They were expected now to make an attempt to occupy the rest —this was the reason behind Admiral Cunningham's order for the "S" class submarines to be moved into the eastern Mediterranean with Beirut as their base.

Seraph stayed for just one day in Beirut before sailing on October 20th, 1943, into the Kaso Straits. These were the last days of the German rearguard stand in the Middle East and the last operational patrol of the war for *Seraph*—though neither was aware of it at the time.

The Dodecanese dotted the eastern Mediterranean; there were dozens of them, some little bigger than the ships that sailed through them. A tiny island itself, Kaso was the largest in *Seraph*'s immediate vicinity, lying close to starboard. Over her horizon, to port, lay Crete, a veritable continent in comparison and securely held by the Germans.

Edsell's charts of the area showed that there was a minefield across the Straits and, obeying the rules of hard experience, *Seraph* dived deep to pass through it. As always, the penetration of an enemy minefield was a frightening business until a numbed fatalism set in and duties were carried out automatically. Occasionally the scrape of a mine's mooring wire across the submarine sent shock rippling through the crew, but otherwise the busiest man aboard was the navigator.

Seraph cleared the minefield in the forenoon of the 26th and came up to periscope depth for a look at Kaso and any shipping which might be lurking in the island's shadows. There was nothing of interest so she moved slowly westwards to occupy a patrol line between two slivers of land called Mayos and Mykoni.

The first sign that Ferdinand the Bull might have to quit

munching buttercups and daisies came six days later in the forenoon watch when a large sail hove in sight from round an island corner. It was a supply caique—a heavily built barge type of boat ranging from fifty up to 100 tons in size, which carried a vast expanse of canvas sail. These vessels were peculiar to the Aegean and most of them had been commandeered by the Germans to run inter-island supply services.

Seraph closed the enemy at periscope depth and saw the crew sunbathing on the deck, obviously not expecting trouble in these waters. He was low in the water, indicating a heavy load and worth sinking. *Seraph* surfaced and fired a shot across his bows. To her astonishment, the crew leapt to their feet and jumped overboard to swim lustily for the nearest shore. In this labyrinth of narrow waterways between islands it was impossible for an average swimmer not to make land in almost any direction.

The caique was raked from stem to stern with binoculars as the submarine closed her slowly, aware that it might turn out to be a "Q" ship—a disguised anti-submarine warship. But all was innocent enough. *Seraph* ranged alongside, threw grappling irons across and a boarding party leapt over. She was the fifty-ton *SY-738* bound from the island of Paros to the north with a consignment of barbed wire for the defence of Mykoni. This was clear evidence that she was working for the enemy.

At Jewell's orders, wads of cotton wool soaked in whale oil were stuffed around her bridge and set alight. When the boarding party had returned, *Seraph* cast off the grappling irons and moved away as Norris tossed a hand grenade on the caique's deck for good measure. It went off with a loud crack and the last seen of Mykoni's first line of defence was a stack of burning crates in a boat hissing her way to the bottom.

Recording this incident in his official report, Jewell said: "I can see now that I was guilty of a tactical mistake then. I could hardly shoot the men on the island and it would have been impractical to take them aboard as prisoners. So I left them where they were confident that one of their friends would soon be along to pick them up. Of course, they were picked up and probably very soon which meant they were able to warn the enemy of our presence. I realise now I should have taken them aboard for the night and sent them ashore on some island well away from the patrol area where they would not have been found so soon."

However, *Seraph* was pleased with her performance. The caique had cost only one grenade and a 3-inch shell but, more important, had given an indication that the Germans were using that part of the world. In not much less than an hour she was to test her strength in a punishing battle and bitterly regret having left that caique crew on their island.

At 12.27 p.m., while hovering at periscope depth in a narrow channel, what at first sight appeared to be two small troop transports steamed slowly towards her. This was a more likely target and she moved across to intercept. Closer inspection revealed the enemy's decks to be crowded with uniformed sailors, but further conjecture was interrupted by Jewell's orders:

"Fire Numbers Two and Three. . . ."

The two torpedoes raced under the mirror-like surface towards the first ship. Then, to Jewell's horror, the track bubbles foamed to the surface with astounding clarity and almost immediately the two vessels altered course sharply towards them. They had seen the tracks from the start and were now racing towards the firing point at high speed with sharp, menacing bows cutting through the flat sea and sending creamy bow waves splaying out to port and starboard.

These were not supply ships or transports but Unterseebootsjaeger—deadly, little destroyers designed for killing submarines in confined waters. The periscope lowered, *Seraph* maintained her depth but increased to maximum speed on her electric motors. Although their deeper, louder hum would be easier to pick up in the enemy's asdic than slow speed, the enemy were more intent on straining to reach the firing point where they hoped the submarine would be than on hunting with listening devices; also it was *Seraph*'s most urgent need at that moment to put as much distance as possible between herself and the hunters in the few minutes left before the depth charges started to call.

She covered nearly 300 yards in the time it took the Germans to travel the mile between them and the first sighting of the torpedo tracks.

General Eisenhower at a S.H.A.E.F. Conference, (*left*) Air Chief Marshal Sir Arthur Tedder and (*right*) General Montgomery, and other Chiefs of Staff.

Officers and crew of *Seraph* with their Jolly Roger. The bars on the top right-hand corner denote successful special operations.

Captain Jewell accompanies Princess Margaret on a recent inspection of ships of the Rhine Flotilla.

(*Below*) Admiral Wright, Commander of U.S. Atlantic Fleet and Supreme Allied Commander, Atlantic (N.A.T.O.).

Astern came the awful "tonk-tonk-tonk" of exploding depth charges and the helmsman, slate and pencil handy, marked up the first score. Now the hunt would begin in earnest. The periscope was raised for Jewell to take a quick look at the direction in which they were searching. He had time to take a mental snapshot of the German Navy uniforms on the fore decks of the two ships pointing straight at him, and then the periscope was lowered again.

He had noted that the first pattern of charges had exploded below the level behind held by *Seraph* and guessed the Germans had assumed that their enemy had dived deep. They would be setting the depth charges even deeper next, thought Jewell. He turned to Scott. "We'll stay at periscope depth, Number One. See if you can catch a stopped trim now."

Scott nodded and gave his orders. All movement through the submarine was banned, the engines cut and the generators disconnected. Scott was the trick cyclist now. He brought the submarine to a stop and, after a few anxious lurches, she remained still, perfectly balanced just below the surface. If one of the crew moved heavily or if depth charges dropped close enough to sway her, she would lose balance, and take a deep plunge or rise suddenly to the surface. Otherwise, she was as safe as she would ever be under attack. Jewell's guess that the Germans would aim deep was confirmed by the next barrage which exploded closer but at least 100 feet deeper.

The hunters were making a lot of noise with their propellers and there would be plenty of warning if they came close. For the moment they were dashing hither and thither some 200 yards away.

Jewell used the long wait to write the rough draft from which he would later take his official Report: "There seems little doubt that these chaps had picked up the stranded caique crew shortly after we left the scene and had come looking for us. I played into their hands by firing the torpedoes. They had been expecting some such attack and every available man aboard each destroyer had been placed on deck to give warning of approaching topedoes."

The helmsman marked up each explosion round the motionless submarine. The loudest sound in the control room was the squeak of the chalk on his slate.

M

After six hours the air began to go foul, stinking sickeningly in their nostrils and coating mouths with a horrid fungus taste. But the destroyers nosed around like scavengers for another two hours before the sea was still outside *Seraph*. It was tempting to poke up the periscope to see if they had gone, but certain that the Germans would be there, lying stopped and hoping to fool the submarine into believing they had given up.

Eight hours and, according to the helmsman's slate, fifty-eight depth charges after the attack had begun there was a sudden roar from above. Tired of hunting such an elusive enemy, the Germans drove off, confident that at least they had driven *Seraph* out of the Aegean.

Half an hour passed before the periscope was cautiously poked up to swivel round the horizon. Nothing disturbed the quiet serenity of the surface; a bright pale moon shone from a cloudless sky and reflected in untroubled waters. They could surface in safety.

Jewell lifted the conning tower "lid" slowly, allowing the bad greenish air to hiss through the widening crack. Had he opened up more quickly the pressure might have thrown him out.

He climbed into the cool, clean night taking large gulps of air to cleanse his lungs. The bridge watch followed and in a few seconds the blowers whirred to life sucking fresh air into *Seraph*'s foul-smelling body.

As though emerging from some strong anæsthetic on the operating table, she came to life. Purified internally, she began to move under the power of the diesels, trembling slightly with their throb; the low chatter of busy men came up softly through the conning tower hatch mingling with the sound of crockery washed and laid. Revived senses reacted hungrily to the sweet smell of fried eggs reminding the crew of healthy appetites. Smoking was permitted and the normal routine quickly established.

The submarine's return to sanity was to be only temporary. Relaxed and at ease one minute, nerves tautened again as a look-out shouted his report: "Aircraft approaching dead ahead, sir."

The sound of engines reached them almost instantly and, starkly revealed on this glorious night, *Seraph* hurried down to seek protection behind a screen of 80 feet of water. The electric motors took over from the diesels and she edged along at six knots conserving precious battery power for the long hunt which the aircraft might bring.

The depth charges began falling, well clear but near enough to convince her she was again under fire. The enemy had reported to base, informed the Luftwaffe and, knowing she would have to come up for air after the surface attack, they had given her time to relax before flying in low to catch her on the surface.

Now the pattern bombing opened in earnest. Unable to see the submarine but knowing where she had dived, the aircraft systematically plastered a "box" around her. As each flight dropped its load and returned to base for more, another took its place. In this way the enemy was able to maintain a continuous shuttle service giving the submarine little peace of mind.

Occasionally, a particularly close barrage jarred her, but her greatest hurt was that she should have been caught like a novice on the surface after the destroyer attack. The aircraft maintained their pounding of the area for the rest of the night, swooping over in an endless chain to drop their loads before returning to join the reloading queue. Eight more hours passed before *Seraph* could hear the enemy no more. The relentless hunt had been kept up now for a total of sixteen hours. Painfully she struggled to the surface, another pillar of foul air rushed from her opened "lid" and the whirring blowers sucked great fresh draughts into her lungs.

It was daylight; brilliant, sun-swept daylight. Friendly rays of warmth reached out protectively to massage life into her aching, wounded body.

The crew had withstood the ordeal well. Now Jewell ordered "Up Spirits" and large tots of rum were handed round to rejuvenate numbed bodies. Then an argument broke out in the engine room where a teetotal sailor bargained with another for his rum ration; and in the manner of British sailors everywhere, a hard, bloody-worded deal was struck causing laughter to ring through the ship. They were back to normal; they could even feel proud to have survived when they looked at the helmsman's slate.

Seraph headed for Samos, the focal island for her new patrol area. Surfaced that night she unexpectedly met friends, two sisters who had been transferred with her from Algiers—*Surf* and *Shakespeare*. The three submarines exchanged pleasantries and information, then drifted apart, each taking up her own position in the general search for enemy targets.

The next five days of island probing produced nothing but frustration. The enemy were by-passing the area, taking no chances and knowing well that *Seraph* might have survived his beating. She steamed back to the Kaso Straits and waited for a target to appear. At midnight on November 5th—an appropriate day on which to seek revenge with guns at the ready—a low, squat supply vessel came in sight heading from the general direction of Crete and probably bound for the enemy base at Leros.

Seraph surfaced, fired the customary shot across the merchantman's bows and closed to investigate, but the enemy altered course away and tried to outpace her. The 3-inch gun lay on the target and opened with rapid fire. The first two shots fell short, the third hit the merchant ship amidships. A flash of red, a brief appearance of flying debris and the enemy stopped, her crew taking to the boats with remarkable agility. This was an astonishing development when the ship had every evidence of being well-armed. Two light guns poked from the bridge, a heavier gun was mounted on the foredeck and one of larger calibre than *Seraph*'s 3-inch jutted from the stern. Cautiously, she approached her prey, ready to blaze into action at the slightest sign of a trap. They could read her name on the stern, *Heraklia*.

Ranging alonside, Jewell could see no sign of life and ordered a boarding party to search her hold and examine the ship's papers. From the main cabin below decks emerged a company of German soldiers—fourteen of them—including two black-uniformed S.S. officers. The crew looked incredulous. All their wartime lives they had been anonymous sinkers of ships, rarely, if ever, meeting the enemy personally. They could remember seeing soldiers dash about the beach at Galita but that was the closest they had been to the enemy in the flesh; now they were close enough to be on speaking terms. More surprising, there had not been even token resistance from such a heavily-armed supply ship.

The fourteen men were quickly bundled aboard *Seraph* and one officer, flanked by the S.S. pair, halted before Jewell on the conning tower, saluted with stiff formality and released a torrent of guttural German. Jewell brusquely beckoned him below with the rest. The boarding party checked the cargo and found a rich harvest of supplies for Leros— diesel oil, lubricating oil, paraffin, two air compressors and welding plants. Jewell considered taking her as a prize, but she would be missed and searched for and that meant providing air cover and escorts. Instead of wasting ammunition or a torpedo on a helpless victim, he called back the boarding party, withdrew and, at the risk of damaging the submarine's nose, rammed the ship amidships. Two rounds of 3-inch were pumped into the superstructure to rekindle the dying fire from the first hit and the supply ship was left listing under the inrush of water.

It was early morning, so *Seraph* dived and Jewell joined his officers below in the patient task of trying to question the Germans. The non-commissioned officers and men had been herded into the torpedo room while the officers were under guard in the secondary wardroom.

After an hour they got little further than discovering that the ship had been bound for the naval and air base at Leros, but the most surprising and satisfying morsel of information was that the important-looking officer was Major Koesch, commander of the area. The S.S. men were his bodyguards with the soldiers as escort. He had been attending a conference at German headquarters in Crete and had returned by ship feeling in need of a holiday.

Curiously, most of these soldiers came from Hamburg which had so long been a target for Bomber Command. They all carried black-bordered postcards from Berlin notifying them that their relatives had been killed during air raids. With these were pictures of their wives and families which they produced readily.

Major Koesch was unmarried but weighed down with pictures of girl friends, some dressed, some in bathing suits and others quite definitely naked. He managed to convey that, as an officer of the German Reich and a handsome one at that, he was extremely popular with the girls at home. He was utterly dismayed at the prospect of a bachelor existence in a prison camp.

Seraph was crowded now, but her patrol was nearly at an end. Jewell had been considering an attack on the near-by naval base of Pegadia for some days and, now that Guy Fawkes night, 1943, had started with a bang, decided to use the remaining hours of darkness to cover an attempt to penetrate the harbour to light a bonfire of his own—singeing Hitler's moustache, so to speak. His sailing orders had mentioned the base as a possible target so he would not be playing truant from his patrol.

Seraph crept across the entrance to Pegadia Bay at 5.30 a.m. but it proved impossible to carry out a proper reconnaissance submerged—and there was too much danger from shore batteries to surface in daylight.

Timing the attack to coincide with dusk while there was still sufficient light for a gun action, *Seraph* surfaced and moved slowly into the harbour. On the sea front was a large yellow building guarded by sentries and surrounded with barbed wire —obviously the enemy headquarters. A heavy gun pointed from behind a screen of sandbags to the left of the house. Further to the left of the beach was a jetty covered with more barbed wire and alongside it a large caique flying the swastika. A smaller caique was anchored nearby and beyond her an Arado seaplane moored to a buoy. There was no evidence that they had been sighted from ashore.

Seraph put on speed, pointed at the large caique and fired one torpedo. Swinging away from this, her 3-inch gun barked into action against the seaplane. A few seconds later it was burning brightly and from the jetty came a huge explosion as the caique disintegrated. By now soldiers were streaming out of the barracks behind the headquarters, and concealed shore batteries opened up from the other side of the bay.

The smaller caique was quickly set alight and then the 3-inch engaged the headquarters ashore. There was a flash of red from the upper floor and smoke began pouring through the windows. A few more shells ensured that it would burn too fiercely to save. At Jewell's command the gun proceeded to shell every building in sight. By now the enemy were getting *Seraph*'s range as she sailed even closer to the shore to give the gunners a chance to destroy the base.

Then the oerlikon gun abaft the bridge joined in the chorus sending tracer balls plummeting into buildings on the other side of the bay. Several rushing, whacking thuds against the conning tower indicated that the enemy machine-gunners had the range, and *Seraph* zig-zagged hurriedly to shake their aim. By now, several buildings were blazing, the two caiques and the seaplane had sunk and it seemed a good time to retire. Delay now might cost *Seraph* her life and make the attack too costly for victory. The battle of Pegadia had lasted twenty exhilarating minutes which had repaid the enemy in full for the punishment inflicted upon *Seraph* six days before.

She headed for her new base at Beirut. The Aegean had not proved an unprofitable operational area and might yield satisfying results in the future. But the accumulated wounds of two severe depth charge attacks had made it imperative to enter dry dock for an overhaul.

EPILOGUE

AT Beirut, reaction set in with disastrous and sudden results. There was no applause when Admiral Cunningham reported: "*Seraph* has made a valuable contribution to the destruction of the enemy in the Aegean theatre." Both crew and ship were indifferent, submerged in a bog of war weariness. Men were jumpy, irritable and in need of leave; also, the ship was sluggish and inclined to halt in her stride with minor breakdowns caused by worn-out machinery.

She was sent on what was thought to be another operational patrol into the Gulf of Athens, but a signal ordered them to proceed to Malta immediately to refuel and collect stores for the passage home to England.

She behaved well crossing the western Mediterranean and, after forty-eight hours at Gibraltar—her first view of the Mediterranean had been the Rock, now it was her last—she sailed into the Atlantic and met weather which gave her a heavy beating as she struggled northward. Exhausted, and with old battle scars breaking open under the effort, she came to rest along the submarine jetty at Chatham on December 23rd, 1943.

By the end of January, the crew were rested and returned to duty in other submarines, other ships and in other bases scattered round the world. There was still a war to be won, battles to be fought and fresh demands to be met. They would not forget the *Seraph* who, refusing to settle down to the endless routine of operational patrols, had led them from one strange adventure to another.

In her they had made friends, from the humblest sailor aboard *Maidstone* to the Supreme Allied Commander, General Eisenhower. But their closest and most affectionate memories would be coupled with their second commanding officer—Captain Jerry Wright to whom they had granted the sole right to call them his men of U.S.S. *Seraph*, and his fellow countrymen, General Mark Clark, General "Lem" Lemnitzer and Colonels Hamblen, Holmes and Gaylord.

In company with Captain Barney Fawkes and Jewell, these

were the men who had met *Seraph* at the beginning of her
career. She had sailed with them under two captains and flying
the Stars and Stripes on missions which had set the pattern
for Anglo-American co-operation in the field.

Mark Clark had told General Eisenhower: "We've had to
rely on the British Navy, their Commandos and the R.A.F.
If the rest are as good as these boys, this war's won."

Captain Fawkes had reported to Sir Andrew Cunningham:
"The friendship and respect the officers and ship's company of
Seraph feel for their distinguished passengers augurs well for
the future success of Anglo-American collaboration."

Since those days, the Americans had rarely missed an
opportunity to show their appreciation of *Seraph* and her crew.
Neither side would easily forget.

Jewell arrived back at his home in Pinner to find that Clark
and Eisenhower had found a way at last to recognise his work on
the North African missions. An official letter from Washington
was waiting, informing him that the President of the United
States had been pleased to award him the Legion of Merit, one
of America's most cherished decorations and the highest the
President is permitted by Congress to award a foreigner.
Another letter from Their Lordships instructed him to report
to the Admiralty from where he would be taken to the London
headquarters of the American Navy in Grosvenor Square.

With a staff captain from the Royal Navy at his side and
senior officers of the American Navy on either flank, the broad
sash of the Legion of Merit was placed round his neck by
Admiral Stark in the name of President Roosevelt.

The citation read:

"The President of the United States of America in accordance with the order issued by General George Washington
at Headquarters, New Burgh, New York, on August 7th, 1782,
and pursuant to Act of Congress, has awarded the Legion of
Merit to Lieutenant Norman Limbury Auchinleck Jewell,
Royal Navy, for extraordinary fidelity and exceptionally
meritorious conduct in the performance of outstanding service
to the Government of the United States as commanding officer
of a British submarine during the assault on the Island of
Sicily.

"After manœuvring his submarine to the proper location,

Lieutenant Jewell steadily maintained his position in spite of enemy searchlights which played on his vessel from the beaches and gave the pre-arranged signals, enabling the units of a Task Force to locate their respective beaches accurately."

This was the same honour given to General Clark for his rôle in the North African operations. It was disclosed later that Jewell was one of the few British officers ever recommended for recognition by General Patton. His report on *Seraph*'s stand during "Operation Husky" had reached Eisenhower who immediately saw an opportunity to reward both Jewell and his ship.

The Admiralty had taken no action to recognise *Seraph* after "Husky", so Eisenhower wrote a report to Washington enclosing Clark's former recommendations.

Shortly after this ceremony, Jewell received the Distinguished Service Cross for his operation patrols in the Western Mediterranean and Aegean. Another important event at that time was his engagement to Rosemary Galloway, then at Allied Forces Headquarters in Italy, who afterwards became his wife.

In February, he returned to Chatham and formally handed *Seraph* over to the dockyard hands. He was told that her wounds were so serious she might never recover. It had been decided to send her to the breaker's yard, the graveyard of ships.

Back in London again, he cabled Jerry Wright in Washington: "Regret to announce impending death of *Seraph*." Being in whimsical mood, he signed it, "Daddy".

Back came the second captain's reply: "My deepest sympathy in your bereavement." It was signed, "Mother".

Seraph's career did not in fact end in 1944. Life persisted in her and she was granted a reprieve—submarines are not thrown aside so carelessly. Having cheated death, she was refitted and ready for sea again in April under a new captain and crew.

She sailed protestingly to the south western approaches of the Channel on a pre-invasion patrol during which an inquisitive enemy aircraft forced her to dive. She dived a little too far and hit bottom at 500 feet, ripping her inside to pieces but only bruising her hull.

Patched up again, she was put out to pasture in the calm

waters of the Clyde at Rothesay where she could rest between training trips for crews manning her younger operational sisters.

Since then her face has been lifted many times with the addition of new equipment; today, she is the oldest submarine in the Royal Navy—the grandmother of the Submarine Service. She lives in Rothesay still and, by acting as a target ship, continues to serve by helping her brood of younger submarines to maintain the high standard of integrity and fitness for instant battle which she had insisted upon in her own youth.

She has been parted from Ferdinand the Bull for many years but through some curious quirk of fortune remains closely associated with her two captains. Commanding the Squadron in which she now serves is Captain Norman Limbury Auchinleck Jewell, D.S.O., M.B.E., D.S.C., R.N., who, from his quarter-deck on H.M.S. *Adamant*, the squadron's depot ship, continues to keep a fatherly eye on her activities in old age.

Jerry Wright, her second captain, is now Admiral Jerauld Wright, U.S.N., Commander-in-Chief of the United States Atlantic Fleet and Supreme Allied Commander (Atlantic) in the NATO organisation. As such he is the Admiral under whom Jewell and *Seraph* would serve in the event of hostilities.

Also attached to *Seraph*'s squadron today are two of her original crew, the former Leading Seamen Hinds and Wiseman, both Chief Petty Officers now and filled with wartime memories —Hinds claims that her former routine of turning night into day and vice versa has affected his sleeping habits.

She will not forget General Clark. On the door leading to the "heads"—naval term for toilet—is a polished brass plaque bearing the inscription: "General Mark Wayne Clark, Deputy Supreme Allied Commander in North Africa, sat here."

It is significant, perhaps, that all the principal characters in the *Seraph* story have now reached or are about to reach the top of their peacetime professions. On the British side, Captain Barney Fawkes became a Rear-Admiral and served for a considerable time as Flag Officer in command of submarines before retiring in the spring of 1956; Bill Jewell is among the youngest full captains in the Royal Navy and at the most interesting stage of his career. Spender and Scott are now Lieutenant-Commanders while Mr. Sutton, the Warrant Engineer, is a Commander.

On the American side, Admiral Wright's present appointment is sufficient evidence of his rapid climb to the top through the rough seas of competition for Flag rank; General Clark has recently retired as a four-star general and is one of the most respected military leaders in his country; Robert Murphy and Julius Holmes are powerful figures inside the State Department; Colonel Brad Gaylord is a captain of industry wielding great influence in the board rooms of his associated companies; and Captain Beaufré, the young Chief-of-Staff to General Giraud, is now a General, commanding the French garrison in Algiers.

France seemed to have forgotten *Seraph*'s unique service in her cause until 1953 when the War Department in Paris suddenly announced the award of the Legion d'Honneur and Croix de Guerre to the two captains of a submarine called *Seraph*—Wright and Jewell.

Neither of them will soon forget the Ship with Two Captains. It was exciting—and it was fun.

INDEX